4/30/99

To Lynne,

may this offer
greater freedom!

Claudia Black

Changing Course

Turning Points To Recovery

Claudia Black, Ph.D., MSW

MAC Publishing
Denver, Colorado

Cover design by Paula Watts.

ISBN No. 0-910223-20-3
"Changing Course," Copyright ©1993 by Claudia Black
Printed in the United States of America. All Rights Reserved.
This book or parts thereof may not be reproduced in any
form without written permission of the author.

Published by
MAC Publishing, 5005 E. 39th Ave., Denver, Colorado, 80207,
(303) 331-0148

In memory of my dad,
Wilmer Dale Clark

Special thanks to

Lynn Bosworth, who read, reread, typed, retyped, proofed, reproofed. Most importantly, thanks for being an integral part of offering feedback. Your compassion for this project and honesty have been vital to me in this writing.

Bonnie Hesse, who worked far beyond her role as editor in time and talent. Thanks for your commitment to this work, but also to the healing of those who have lived with abandonment, fear and shame. You made a difference.

Contents

3. Four Steps To Freedom

The Process Of Recovery From Chronic Loss

Step One: Explore Past Losses* Grief Work* A Cognitive
Life Raft And Emotional Safety Net* Fear Of Feelings*
Overcoming The Fear Of Feelings* Step Two: Connect
The Past To Present Life* Step Three: Challenge Inter-
nalized Beliefs* Step Four: Learn New Skills* Applying
The Four Steps To A Recovery Issue* Recovery Can't
Be Rushed

4. Building Your Own Inner Adult

Skills To Create A Core Of Personal Strength

Creating An Inner Holding Environment* Core Recovery
Skills* Validating Yourself* Letting Go Of Some Control*
Feeling Your Feelings* Identifying Your Needs* Setting
Limits And Boundaries* Creating A Core Of Strength With
The Recovery Skills

5. The House We Lived In

No More Roles, No More Secrets

Recasting Your Role* Family Secrets* Family Stories*
Identifying Family Roles* Who Am I, If I'm Not Who I've
Been?* Ending Old Roles

6. Recovery Is The Road To Yourself

New Ways Of Being, New Ways Of Relating

Beginning New Relationships* Sharing Your Pain/Grief With Family Members* Confrontation As A Part Of Sharing, As A Way To Ending The Source Of The Pain* How Can I Share My Pain If My Parent Has Died?* Present Day Relationships* Levels Of Relationships* Characteristics Of A Healthy Relationship* "Charting" The Characteristics Of A Healthy Relationship

7. Spirituality Is Something You Are

Forgiving, Loving, Finding Serenity

Spirituality And Control* Spirituality And The Fear Of Abandonment* Spirituality And Forgiveness* Spirituality And Our Religious Upbringing* Spirituality And The Spirit Of Our Inner Child* Practicing Spirituality* Spirituality, The Turning Point To A New Course

Turning Points To Recovery

1
Changing Course

Turning Points to Recovery

"I don't know when my parents began their war against each other, but I do know the only prisoners they took were their children. When [we] needed to escape, we developed a ritual—we found a silent soothing world where there was no pain, a world without mothers and fathers. But that was a long time ago, before I chose not to have a memory."

—Pat Conroy, *The Prince of Tides*

"Forgiving is not forgetting. It is remembering and letting go."

—Claudia Black, *It's Never Too Late to Have a Happy Childhood*

"I've spent my whole life trying to take the pain out of everyone else's life! The whole time, the issue was my pain, not theirs. Today I don't run scared. I know my fear, my hurt, my anger. I also know my joy. Today I don't live in shame."

—Lynn

"Fear and loneliness were all I ever knew—I think I came into this world scared. But now, at forty-two it's different. I no longer medicate my feelings. I've slowed down to be able to meet myself. And I realize I am okay. I am more than okay! I actually look forward to each day."

—Joe

"I wanted so badly to be loved, but for years all I felt was ignored and unwanted. I went to every length possible to make people love me, only to be repeatedly ignored and unwanted. Then, slowly, with the understanding of what had happened in my life and with the freedom to talk about it, things started to turn around. I learned to love myself. What a revelation!"

—Judy

These three people endured decades of pain and then discovered a different way of being in this world, a different way of living their lives. Why did they have pain? How did it go away? and What was the turning point for them? How did they change the course of their lives? These are some of the questions we will try to answer here.

When we grow up with fear and shame, we become adults who live with fear and shame. Accompanying these intense feelings is a pervasive, chronic sense of loss, ranging anywhere from serious to profound. The sensation of this loss goes by various names—unhappiness, hopelessness, depression, emptiness, insecurity, anxiety, boredom. Whatever the words we use, the wound we have has troubled our very spirit. We need to let go of the fear and shame. We need to change our course by putting the cause of our pain in its proper perspective.

What you might personally feel, and how much you feel in the present, depends on what your feelings were back then, when the original wounding began, compounded by your life experiences from that time on. Still, it is difficult to look back. Whatever caused the loss must be pretty bad, you assume, or it wouldn't make you feel so awful—like you're not worth much, if anything; or you haven't really achieved anything of value; or you've never quite done enough; or any good points you have would be negated if people knew the parts of yourself you kept secret.

What is it exactly that we lost? Why do we feel something was missing? Some of us know all too well. For us, life in our early years was organized around our mother's drinking, and the embarrassment, the shame. Or our brother's dying, and the fear, stigma, and prevailing sadness we endured. Or our father's rigid religious fervor, and the shame, confusion, guilt, and anger we felt. Or our parents' outright abandonment of their parenting role and us, their children. Or our physical or sexual abuse by someone who was supposed to love us.

What we lost were the conditions necessary for us to thrive, to grow up according to our own nature. We lost the opportunity to be ourselves—to become who we are. We lived as characters in someone else's drama, a story of his or her war against pain. The family spotlight was nearly always on that other person, and we were merely bit players, "lesser lights" whose characters were never developed in the family script. The lines we were supposed to speak and our range of emotions were limited, so that we didn't conflict with the main character who, in essence, stole the show.

Many others of us resonate to the idea of chronic loss, but we can't put our finger on anything specific that happened—no identifiable abuse, addiction, or other blatant dysfunction in our lives. No tragic figure to shoulder the blame. In our case, the loss was "growing in the shadow," the shadow of our parents' pain from their own chronic loss. Extending the drama analogy and factoring in what we know now, we would probably see that our parents themselves had been character actors in someone else's play and that, in many ways, the other play is still going on off-stage in the wings of our lives, as it were. As a result, what happened in our families was far less obvious, but we were affected nonetheless.

Whether we grew up in a subtly or blatantly painful family, we learned to push our concerns aside and stuff our feelings away, because we felt guilty, weak, and ashamed that we felt such loss, fear, and shame.

LIVING BY THE RULES:

Don't Talk, Don't Trust, Don't Feel

I have this great job. I travel. I'm self-sufficient. Maybe I don't need to be able to get closer to people."

"I'm fifty-two years old. Why should I be angry with my dad for being a victim of his era? All dads hit their kids once in a while. So my dad made bruises! My life isn't so bad."

"My mother created a lot of pain in my life, being so critical and acting like a jealous girlfriend, but she was also all I had. It could have been worse."

These skeptics may be correct—there are others who had it worse. But, the fact that others had it worse doesn't take away your loss. There will always be a greater horror story. Your loss is not negated by someone else's. Your loss is your own pain.

How do you go from living according to the rules, Don't Talk, Don't Trust, Don't Feel, to a life where you are free to talk and trust and feel? You do this through a process that teaches you to go the source of those old, transgenerational rules, to question them and to recreate new rules of your own. You will also have to grieve what is now past, but has left you with pain. As you go through this process of renewal, you will discover that your life will change course as a result. You will learn new ways to think about old experiences and beliefs; learn new processes for feelings, positive and negative, past and present; and learn new skills, new behaviors toward yourself and others.

GOING BACK TO THE PAST

"My friends have given me all the books, but I don't want to touch those issues."

"I'm twenty-three. I want to move on in my life. Why all this recovery stuff?"

"Why would I want to talk about that now? It was a long time ago."

Why do I have to go back to the past? you ask. Why are you reluctant to? one wonders in response. Whenever we resist, there's a reason. People who resist going back to face difficult childhood issues are not fully acknowledging the pain of the loss or trauma that occurred in their lives. When they resist recovery, they aren't perceiving the value of addressing what they feel. In addition, these people have used defenses to avoid facing their pain—workaholism, excessiveness in sexual or eating behaviors, perfectionism or extreme caretaking, for instance. These behaviors are often culturally supported, causing some people to question why they should want to recover from behaviors that are seen as "good" versus "bad."

HOW DO YOU RECOVER WHAT YOU'VE NEVER HAD?

While you can't re-live those early years, you can recover from the pain of the past—gradually. And little by little, you can let down those defenses that once helped you survive, but are actually hurting you now. You can learn new life skills so you can begin to accept and internalize that it is truly possible for you...

... to be imperfect and still be lovable;

... to make mistakes and still be forgiven;

.. to feel and express your feelings openly, honestly, safely.

No more secret shame. No more need to make a superhuman effort to stay in control so you can keep up appearances, protecting your vulnerability and hiding your true self from others. No more need to put up barriers that keep people at a distance.

This new way of living is possible for those who choose it whenever they choose it. Yes, you are young. Yes, you are middle-aged. Yes, you are older. Whatever your age, recovery is there if you want it. It takes recognizing that you'd like at least part of your life to be different than it is now. You'd like less of something, you'd like more of something else.

The turning point in your life comes with a new awareness:

"There is another reality than the one I live. I want it."

Then a new willingness:

"I am willing to take some risks to have it."

This book will offer a framework for understanding the recovery/ healing process from childhood family pain that has carried forward in your life, and fostered beliefs and behaviors that have perpetuated your pain. We will identify specific steps in recovery, examine the core issues you will face, and offer guidelines regarding expectations for yourself and others you care about. First, however, we will look the meaning of the term "Adult Child."

"ADULT CHILD"

"Adult Child" means that within an adult frame is a person who has survived harmful events and conditions in his/her family of origin. This survivor is tough, but has carried much pain. Within this person there is a stifled inner spirit, a still-wounded inner child—one who has been hurt and who now needs to be recognized, validated, and healed. Many people have not yet reached the turning point to healing, and so haven't begun to change the course of their lives. These adult-age people feel as emotionally vulnerable as nine-year-old or twelve-year-old children. That does not mean they behave as children, but that they are adults who have carried the pain of their loss all their lives. I picture an Adult Child as a nine-year-old with thirty-five years of pain or a twelve-year-old with forty-five years of pain. To date, the oldest person I have worked with on Adult Child issues was eighty-six; another was eighty-two. So, really, a person of any age whose family of origin was characterized by chronic loss or trauma is an Adult Child who can recover.

It is important for you to know that the term "Adult Child" is not meant to act as a label that limits who you are, but to provide a helpful way to speak to your unhealed pain. Also, there is no certain degree of family stress or type of family loss that "adds up" to being an Adult Child. Instead, all of our lives can be viewed on a continuum from "No Pain" to "All Pain," and the combined effect of our experiences, past and present, falls somewhere between these extremes. There is no amount you must have suffered in order to have permission to heal.

If you have pain, you deserve to heal.

If you have anger or guilt from the past, you deserve to heal.

If you are protecting yourself from past pain in ways that are causing you even more pain in the present, you deserve to heal.

When you are able to accept these truths, you will reach a turning point that will change the course of your life.

At birth, a child has a "bill of human rights." A child has the right to be loved for who he or she is rather than for being what others wish him/her to become; the right to be nurtured and parented rather than to make up for the parents' losses; the right to consistency, security, warmth and understanding; the right to unconditional love; the right to be protected from traumatic situations.

Yet, for children raised in troubled families, these basic rights are lost. Instead, they must struggle for the right merely to survive. As a consequence of their loss, these adult-age individuals have difficulty experiencing a healthy life until the child within each of them is able to speak the truth about their childhoods and free themselves from the bondage of the past. Until this recognition and healing occurs, Adult Children are doomed to live a life without choice, reliving old pain and controlling the pain in old ways. Unless something changes, they are characters trapped in their old life dramas, destined to live out old scripts.

THE TROUBLED FAMILY

A family's life together is troubled when the conditions that foster physical and emotional growth and well-being are continuously absent over time. The absence of these nurturing conditions has the cumulative effect of creating a childhood experience of CHRONIC LOSS and ABANDONMENT. Within a family, the dynamics that create a sense of loss are DENIAL, RIGIDITY, ISOLATION, and SHAME. Everyone will experience these things sometimes, or occasionally, but when children experience denial, rigidity, isolation, and shame on an ongoing basis, they carry forward an overriding sense of chronic loss. How chronic loss is created is illustrated on the following chart, "The Experience Of Pain From A Child's Point of View."

CHRONIC LOSS AND ABANDONMENT

Some Loss Is Necessary; Some Is Not

We all experience loss in our life. From birth we embark on a journey of individuation from our fathers and mothers. This is the process of giving up what we must to become separate human beings. The losses we experience as a result are natural or "necessary losses" and are balanced by gains that build our strength and health.

Children naturally experience loss of some level of security as they enter school. There is a sense of loss when children move to a new area and a new home. They experience another kind of natural loss through the death of a loved one, whether it is a family member, friend, or a pet.

A common natural loss is that of a pet. This is a painful time, and often is a child's first experience with death. As painful as that can be, it is less so in our father's or mother's arms. In a troubled family, though, children are often not supported in their pain or told not to show what they feel; sometimes they're also told not to feel what they feel—to keep a stiff upper lip, to stop crying—to stop acting like a child. In a severely dysfunctional family, the scenario might be that one parent intentionally causes the loss—for example, by giving away your cat—and the other parent denies the significance of what happened, maybe even denies that it happened at all. When we experience a natural loss and are supported by our parents, we feel sad, but loved and secure. When we are not supported, we feel sad, unloved and abandoned. This lack of support or help with our pain is, then, an abandonment experience.

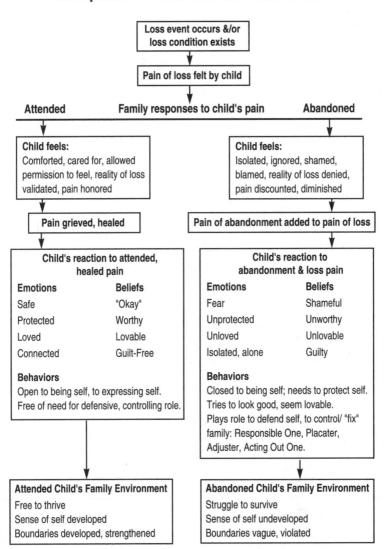

How Chronic Loss Is Created
The Experience of Pain from a Child's Point of View

Loss event occurs &/or
loss condition exists

↓

Pain of loss felt by child

↓

Attended   Family responses to child's pain   **Abandoned**

Child feels:
Comforted, cared for, allowed
permission to feel, reality of loss
validated, pain honored

Child feels:
Isolated, ignored, shamed,
blamed, reality of loss denied,
pain discounted, diminished

Pain grieved, healed   Pain of abandonment added to pain of loss

Child's reaction to attended, healed pain		Child's reaction to abandonment & loss pain	
Emotions	**Beliefs**	**Emotions**	**Beliefs**
Safe	"Okay"	Fear	Shameful
Protected	Worthy	Unprotected	Unworthy
Loved	Lovable	Unloved	Unlovable
Connected	Guilt-Free	Isolated, alone	Guilty

Behaviors
Open to being self, to expressing self.
Free of need for defensive, controlling role.

Behaviors
Closed to being self; needs to protect self.
Tries to look good, seem lovable.
Plays role to defend self, to control/ "fix"
family: Responsible One, Placater,
Adjuster, Acting Out One.

Attended Child's Family Environment
Free to thrive
Sense of self developed
Boundaries developed, strengthened

Abandoned Child's Family Environment
Struggle to survive
Sense of self undeveloped
Boundaries vague, violated

Pain of loss + pain of abandonment = an abandonment experience.
Chronic abandonment experiences = chronic loss.
CHRONIC LOSS for a child = loss of conditions for thriving.

Abandonment Is Not A Necessary Loss

"Oh sure, I remember the first day of school. Don't we all? My seven-year- old sister woke me up yelling. She dressed me while Mom was sleeping. Dad was away. She held my hand, took me to her school, and told me to stay away from the older kids and not to fall asleep."

"Two different times growing up my father actually gave our dogs away—our pets! My best friends! My parents told us both times that they were killed by cars, but I overheard Mom telling Grandma the real story!"

"I remember my graduation. My dad was too busy to get there until it was over."

These are examples of children who were emotionally abandoned. They were not offered solace, direction, and support at significant times in their lives. Not only are many of us not offered protection at times of natural loss, it is often true we may be in families that create losses for children. What is most damaging is that those losses take place at the time in life when we are developing our self-worth.

These losses are most often due to emotional abandonment, physical abandonment ,or both. Emotional abandonment occurs when the parent, or primary caretaker, is not consistently emotionally available to the child. While physical needs are being met, there is little or no nurturing, hugging, or emotional intimacy developing between the parent and the child. The unnecessary losses a child experiences may range from loss of quality and quantity of time with a parent, loss of childhood as a result of unrealistic expectations placed on the child, loss of hope, loss of opportunity, to loss of innocence.

"By the time I was seven, I was the little adult at home. I had to be perfect. There was no laughter, no fun, no tenderness."
"After my third foster home, I knew no one was coming for me."

"My dad didn't care about me. He clearly liked being away from

home better than he liked us kids. By the time I was eleven, I didn't care much about things either. No one had time for me, so what did it matter if I was a screw-up."

Loss is not always a result of what does happen; sometimes loss is the result of what does not happen, or what you don't have that you need. It may be what you did not hear from a parent, such as "I love you" or "You are special." The loss could also be a result of what you didn't get to say because your parents weren't available, or what you didn't get to do with them, i.e., play, work on projects. Words and time are important to all children as they grow up. They convey to us that we are valued.

Physical abandonment occurs when a child has repetitively missed meals, has been left alone for hours or days unsupervised, or has been left without adequate supervision. Due to our ability to deny, we sometimes negate our abandonment. "I was always supervised. Maybe Mom and Dad weren't home, but my older brother was." Although being left with older siblings for lengthy periods of time may illustrate one child's valiant effort to protect another child, it still constitutes abandonment by parents. In spite of the maturity of our nine-, twelve-, or fifteen-year-old siblings, they are still nine, twelve or fifteen. We needed adult supervision and protection. Not being properly clothed, not having physical protection are forms of abandonment. Physical and sexual abuse are major boundary violations, acts of physical abandonment when the child is treated as an object and not as a person. Those who are responsible for you owe it to you to see that you are not violated. You deserve protection. Not feeling secure, protected, safe, both psychologically and physically, creates the greatest loss for children. The messages heard by the child experiencing emotional abandonment and physical abandonment are very similar: "You are not of value, you are not wanted, you are in the way."

Being in a family where there is chronic loss affects all of us who were raised that way. It is traumatic to our ability to feel good about ourselves and the world. It can interfere with developing skills that lead to connecting and bonding. It will be significant in the creation of internalized fear and shame.

DENIAL

The Loss Of Natural Openness And Honesty

Denial is a defense mechanism, a natural response to protect against pain. When someone feels helpless to impact their situation and/or is ashamed of what is occurring, they often resort to denial. Denial can be identified when individuals discount, minimize, or rationalize their feelings. As a nine-year-old put it, "Denial is pretending things are different than how they really are." While the word *denial* is most often associated with the addictive family, it is the central dynamic of any dysfunctional system.

To be raised with denial is to know the Rule of Silence. As children we learned that it was not okay to speak our truth and, instead, we should pretend things were different than they were. It may be that our perceptions were not validated, or we felt threatened about speaking up for fear of the consequences or punishment. We may have felt hopeless, believing that nothing good would come from talking. As children raised with the Rule of Silence, we became confused about loyalty. Often we didn't speak up because we were afraid we wouldn't be believed. As upset, frightened, or concerned as we were, we believed that we would jeopardize our well-being and betray those we loved if we spoke our truth.

If we were raised with others close to us also subscribing to the Rule of Silence, we had no practice trusting that those we spoke to would hear us. Many of us just didn't know what to say. We couldn't make sense of people's behavior. We didn't understand or know what was really happening and we had no language to describe it. What we knew most were our feelings, and it was made clear to us that we weren't supposed to talk about them.

Growing up with denial makes it easy to be in denial today and not know it. We discount our feelings and perceptions. We rationalize hurtful behaviors. Today, we may say we aren't angry, disappointed or hurt when we are. We tell ourselves something isn't important when it is. We even tell ourselves certain things don't happen much when they occur frequently. We don't speak our truth. When we spend years learning to minimize, discount, or rationalize, it's only normal to continue to do so as adults. We are so skilled in denying that we do it without conscious thought.

RIGIDITY

The Loss Of Natural Order And Natural Disorder

Troubled families also live with rigidity. Whatever the initial or primary cause of the trouble, whether an abusive parent or an alcoholic grandparent, the problem has made that person's life unmanageable and, to the degree we are affected, our lives are unmanageable. Unmanageable lives are chaotic lives and we do not thrive on chaos. As a result, we respond by creating a rigid, unreal order; yet, we do not thrive on extreme rigidity either, with no allowance for the very real, natural differences between all of us. But, until something intervenes, this order may become a code of beliefs and behaviors handed down for generations.

In troubled families parents were often dogmatic in their thinking: "Things will be this way and there are no exceptions." The old adage, "Children are to be seen and not heard" was often adhered to. Inherent in this stance are Don't Question, and Don't Think rules. This is a family where it is never okay to ever challenge authority. Under the guise of respect you are quietly to submit.

Often, the rigidity was evident in the structure that was imposed on the children. While children need consistency, rigid controls are discouraging and debilitating. *"We weren't allowed out of the house outside of school and church. We couldn't have friends in. We always had chores or had to be doing school work even when there was none to do."* There may have been a lack of fairness regarding family rules and expectations. Parents were unrealistic, expecting far too much from their children. They weren't age, appropriate in their expectations, i.e., expecting a six-year- old to do what is more normal for a twelve-year-old. As a consequence of growing up with rigidity, we as adults are often rigid in our thinking and can't perceive choices. We are unrealistic with ourselves and others.

ISOLATION

The Loss Of Natural Connection And Validation

Emotional isolation is also an integral experience for children in troubled families. Isolation is particularly damaging because we need a connection with others to create meaning in life. Yet we live life as if in a bubble shouting, "Hello out there—I'm alive in here! Does anybody hear me?" but no one answers.

We have learned to live with emotional isolation as a result of not being able to speak the truth. Shelley, age thirteen, depicts the isolation others of us know so well. When asked to draw a picture of her home, she did, showing her bedroom and the living room amplified in size. In the living room the parents were portrayed to be in a heated argument; there were footprints running from the living room to a bedroom where you then saw Shelley and her two sisters hiding at opposite ends of the room from each other behind separate beds. Even in crisis the sisters were unable to connect, to bond, to be of support to each other.

The emotional isolation within the home often carries over to those outside of the family as well. We don't want others to know of our personal pain or the family pain. We are afraid of how others would respond if they knew. As adults, we have come to be socially isolated or capable of surrounding ourselves with others, yet withholding our true feelings and thoughts. The family rules, Don't Talk, Don't Trust, Don't Feel, create our isolation. While we may have social graces, our hallmark is superficiality.

SHAME

The Loss Of Unconditional Security And Self-Worth

When shame is internalized, it becomes the foundation of a

person's trauma. When our parents do not accept who we are and the reality we know, we feel abandoned. The prospect of being abandoned terrifies us because we often equate abandonment with death. Physically, as infant humans, we can't meet our basic needs for food, shelter, and protection. Emotionally, we can't meet our needs for love and nurturing. And, as we grow a little older, it seems only logical that if our very own providers and protectors of life—our parent —don't want us, we must not be worth anything to anybody. Something must be terribly wrong with us if we are worthless to those we love!

Shame is the painful feeling that comes with the belief there is something inherently wrong with who you are. It is the belief that you, or a part of you, is defective or inadequate. Words that describe shame are reflective of seeing oneself as "bad," "ugly," "stupid," "incompetent," "damaged."

To live with shame is to feel alienated and defeated, never quite good enough to belong. It is an isolating experience that makes us think we are completely alone and unique in our unlovableness. It is a feeling that we are intensely and profoundly unlovable. Secretly, we feel like we are to blame. Any and all deficiency lies within ourselves. Gershen Kaufman, author of *Shame, The Power of Caring*, said that "shame, is without parallel, a sickness of the soul." Shame reflects an internal darkness in one's soul. And it is because of this our recovery truly has spiritual meaning.

Underneath layers of shame, you'll find that abandonment is at the foundation. Abandonment, as described earlier, may be emotional or physical. But abandonment is most often experienced through various forms of rejection, rejection that has been colored by parental words and actions, some subtle, some not so subtle. It is useful to visualize a continuum, with acceptance at one end, rejection at the other end, and many shades of parental indifference or emotional unavailability somewhere between. The in-between areas encompass the many ways a child can feel ignored or invalidated by the parent's non-accepting or rejecting behaviors. Whether or not the parent's intention is abandonment, the child feels unloved and undervalued. And, remember, the child is reacting to parents whose job it is to protect, care for and love us. If they reject us in any way, we know in our hearts we must not be worthy.

No one's family is perfect; parents are people who, like everyone else, have weaknesses and faults, and often make mistakes. But when children live with chronic loss resulting from a mixture of rigidity, denial, isolation, and shame, there are many unhealed wounds from which they seek recovery.

LOOKING AT OUR EXPERIENCES OF LOSS

Creating A Loss Graph

To get a more concrete picture of the losses in your life, it may be helpful for you to create a "loss graph." A "loss graph" is a way for you to record those significant losses where your pain can still be felt; it has never gone away. We all experience loss in life, but some of us were very young and/or didn't have the support or the skills to be able to attend to and grieve the pain, and so that pain continues to impact us. Whether your loss was an event or a prevailing condition in your family, if your pain was unattended, you felt abandoned.

The following loss graphs are examples that have been constructed for "Joyce" and "Tim," to help you begin your own. These graphs relate specifically to losses in growing-up years. Losses in adult years will be discussed later.

Loss Graph For Early Years

Joyce

Loss Events:	Grandmother died	Best friend moved	Parents divorced	Family dog died
Age:	7	10	11	15
Unattended Feelings:	Sad, scared	Sad, lonely unloved	Guilty, angry	Sad, alone
Loss Conditions in Family:	Mother depressed; Mother always in bed;	Abandonment Experiences/Feelings:		Guilty for mother's crying; Angry because alone;

Father always at work.   No one came to my school
                                          events; Afraid to bring
                                          friends home; Guilty, believ
                                          ing I'm at fault; Unloved.

Joyce's loss events can be considered fairly common. However, because of the loss conditions in her family, with her parents being unavailable to comfort her and help her feel secure and safe, her abandonment experiences left her with feelings of low self-worth.

Loss Graph For Early Years

Tim

	Brother died in car accident		
Loss Events:	Tim broke arm & leg	Changed to	Vietnam
	Missed half school year	new jr. high	service
Age:	7	12	18-21
Unattended Feelings:	Terror, sadness lonely anger (Dad was driver)	Scared, angry	Fear, powerlessness
Loss Conditions in Family:	Father, angry alcoholic, Mother martyr, Mother continually blamed father for accident; Parents constantly idealized deceased brother.	Abandonment Experiences/Feelings:	Never good enough compared to brother;worthlessness Chronic fear of dying (not protected by parents); Never a sense of safety from war experience.

Tim's losses may have caused deeper wounds than Joyce's, especially his brother's death and his Vietnam experiences. Still, if he had had family support and love, he would have had an opportunity to attend to and grieve his pain. But, Tim also had an overlay of family loss conditions, leaving him even more helpless to attend to his feelings. Consequently, his pain was heightened by his feelings of fear, powerlessness, and inadequacy.

It is important to identify your losses. Here is the format for a loss graph. In the appendix there is an enlarged form for you to fill out.

Loss Graph For Early Years

Loss Events: _____
Age:
Unattended Feelings:

Loss Conditions	Abandonment
In Family:_____	Experiences/Feelings: _____
_____	_____
_____	_____

To begin your loss graph, note the loss events that immediately come to your mind without trying to judge whether or not you are still affected. Record your age and any feelings you remember having had at the time.

Next, note losses you remember related to chronic conditions within your family, such as those which resulted in your feelings of inadequacy, shame, fear, loss of control, loss of innocence, loss of childhood. Sometimes these losses are due to addiction and abuse; many times they are not, but they are nonetheless painful. If you are unable to easily identify family conditions, you may find it helpful to ask: "What was I afraid of? Ashamed of?" Don't force this. Be aware that some people have more easily identified issues than others. Until losses and pain are dealt with directly, the resulting feelings, while often masked, are carried into adulthood. Unless we have a chance to learn healthy coping skills, this combination of past loss and pain leads to severe consequences creating even more pain in the present. Our past-driven, present pain will be explored in the next chapter.

THE IMPACT OF OUR LOSSES

Can we live with these dynamics of loss and not be affected? No. We are all impacted. While families have many common characteristics, there are all kinds of experiences that create differences, and some of us are certainly impacted more negatively than others. There are many variables that create differences in the ways and the depth we feel the effect:

— Age at onset of trauma or loss. The younger we are, the more

hurtful it is to us.
— Stigma associated to dynamics. If stigma is attached, there are greater emotional consequences; i.e., there is greater stigma being in an abusive family than a home characterized by workaholism. — Connection to outside support system. Connection to extended family, friend's family, extra-curricular school activities, the ability to find meaningful relationships, and/or activities outside of family lessens our shame.
— Multiple trauma/shame related dynamics. For example, to live with both addiction and abuse is more traumatic than to live with just one source of pain. [My book *Double Duty* specifically addresses these issues.]

RESILIENCY

We also know that survival skills we learned and developed have helped to create important, personal strengths. To bring about order and predictability in our young lives, to lessen hurtful feelings and defend against pain, we developed skills that have brought a resourcefulness to our personalities. We may have learned to take charge, make decisions, and initiate; we may have learned to be creative, possibly patient; we may have developed a sense of humor.

In spite of trauma, loss, and pain in our growing-up years, we were often given gifts by our parents. We come from these families with a matrix of strengths and vulnerabilities.

Let us not reinstate the Don't Talk rule, though, by discounting the pain, all for the sake of recognizing how strong we are. Owning the trauma that occurred in our lives in no manner lessens the strengths we have developed.

CHANGING COURSE

If you are strong now, why would you want to change? Many people are confused or reluctant about the concept of recovery, thinking it is just another form of giving up themselves and giving in. Recovery does not mean giving up who you are—it means letting go of who you are not.

It means letting go of your pain. You are not your pain.

It means letting go of an undesirable family script. You are no longer an unwitting character in someone else's life, not now that you understand you have the freedom to choose.

Each insight into your past and its connection to your present is like turning on the light in a dark room. It doesn't change what is there, but now that you can see where you are going, you can go in and out freely without harm. Fear no longer drives you—freedom moves you.

Each of these awarenesses bring you new choices.

Each new awareness is a turning point.

TURNING POINT:

There is another reality than the one I live.
I want it.

2
You Can't Go Forward Without Finishing The Past

Healing The Pain Of Abandonment, Fear, And Shame

"In this dream I was stationed underground, in the grave....This was my company, my life, my mission — to watch over the bones. And then slowly... I walked away and climbed out of the grave, into the sun and the wide expanse of the world....I turned one last time to say good-bye. The vigil of the bones was over."

—John, Adult Child of an Alcoholic,
Quoted by Stephanie Brown, *Safe Passages*

"To free yourself from the past you must break the rules of silence and compliance."

—Claudia Black, *It's Never Too Late to Have a Happy Childhood*

When children are raised with chronic loss, without the psychological or physical protection they need, and certainly deserve, it is most natural for them to internalize incredible fear. Not having the necessary psychological or physical protection equals abandonment. And, living with repeated abandonment experiences creates shame. Shame arises from the painful message implied in abandonment: "You are not important. You are not of value." Both the pain of the past, as yet unresolved, and pain in the present created by past-driven behaviors fuel our fear of abandonment and shame. This is the pain from which we need to heal.

PAIN FROM THE PAST

Physical Abandonment

For some children abandonment is primarily physical. Physical abandonment occurs when parents do not provide the physical conditions necessary for thriving, such as:

—lack of appropriate supervision.

—inadequate nutrition and meals provided. There was a book titled *Potato Chips for Breakfast*, and a talk by educator and lecturer Don Bartlette called "Macaroni at Midnight"; these titles so poignantly reflect the poor eating habits of children in some families.

—inadequate clothing, housing, heat, or shelter.

—physical and/or sexual abuse.

As children, we are totally dependent on our caretakers to provide safety in our environment. When they do not, we grow up believing that the world is an unsafe place, that people are not to be trusted, and that we do not deserve positive attention and adequate care.

Emotional Abandonment

Emotional abandonment occurs when parents do not provide the emotional conditions and emotional environment necessary to growing up freely, in accordance with the child's own nature. Because more people experience emotional abandonment than physical abandonment and because it is a more subtle dynamic, the following abandonment experiences may be helpful to understanding emotional abandonment:

—Children have to hide a part of their beings in order to be accepted. Many children experience rejection when they make mistakes and are less than perfect, or when they express needs, show

feelings, or when they have successes. All of these experiences could be met by disapproval, rejection, or even punishment.
—Children cannot live up to the expectations of their parents. These expectations are often unrealistic and not age-appropriate.
—Children are held responsible for other people's behavior. They may be consistently blamed for the actions and feelings of their parents.
—Disapproval is shown toward children that is aimed at their entire beings or identity rather than a particular behavior. Who the child is, is not separated out from what the child does.

Abandonment and Boundaries

Many times our abandonment issues are fused with distorted, confused, or undefined personal boundaries. We experience abandonment when parents have a distorted sense of boundaries, both their boundaries and ours.

When parents do not view us as separate beings with distinct boundaries and find value in us as such, we will experience abandonment. They want us to like what they like, dress like they dress, and feel as they do. This is particularly painful during our teenage years when it is only normal in our development to seek out behaviors different from the parent's as a part of the process of developing and knowing our own self. While this teenage/parent struggle is common to many, some parents cannot recognize this as part of the adolescent stage, but see it as a personal affront to their image, their own source of worth. If we in any way express differences from our parents, or make different choices than they would, we know we run the risk of rejection.

When parents expect us to be extensions of themselves, fulfilling their dreams, we will feel abandoned. How many of us went to the school our father wanted to go to, but wasn't able to? How many entered into careers that our parents chose for us? How many of us married who we did, when we did because that was expected or desired by our parents? I offer a caution in that having done what our parents expected, wanted, or demanded does not mean that it was the wrong thing to do. It just so often means that the decision was never totally ours. It is the process that is more painful or possibly wrong, not necessarily the outcome.

Judy told how her mother spoke as if it were simply fact that neither of her daughters were to have children when they reached childbearing age due to the possibility of transmitting a terminal genetic disease. "My mom made it clear that it was not an option. Because that decision seemed based in her wanting to protect us from pain, and to protect a child from having to die, it was hard to want to question this dictate. Mom's motivation was sincere. But I was twenty-nine years old when I realized I had never made my own decision about this. Until then it had been my mother's dictate. I realized I had to sit down and separate my life choices from my mother's pain in having a child who died young. I wrestled with the decision for a few years and ultimately made the decision to not have a child. Today, the decision is mine, not my mother's."

Certainly, many people do exactly what their parents *don't* want them to do. Often this is a part of their attempt to be able to be a separate person. We don't marry the person our father so liked. We don't go to the college our mother aspired to attend. And often we choose to marry the person they would like the least and simply choose to not attend college at all. Again it is not the outcome that is the issue, as much as it is the decision-making process. Instead of choosing freely, we make a reactive decision based in anger.

When parents are not willing to take responsibility for their feelings, thoughts, and behaviors, but expect us to take responsibility for them, we will experience abandonment. When parents hold children responsible for what should be their responsibility, they are expecting something impossible for a child. In effect, they are telling children that they have more power than, in fact they have, setting them up to experience futility and inadequacy.

When parents' self-esteem is derived through our behavior, their needs override ours, and so once again, we feel abandoned. Henri still feels pain when he talks about how his father publicly gloated over Henri's accomplishments. "Some people told me I should be grateful that my dad even noticed what I was involved in. But there was as always something missing about his being proud of me. When I was growing up, I did well in school, I was a very good athlete. I was a student leader and often had my picture in the local paper. My dad came to my events, boasting about me in a way that never seemed real. His boasting was so grand and his need for people to know it was his son was so strong. Yet there was this total lack of interest in me when I was home. When I got home from the ball games, he would already be in bed. He never boasted to me. He never once congratulated me or patted me on the back."

As readers, we can each interpret Henri's situation differently. What is important to note is that Henri did not get the validation he needed to feel special, of value, and important to his father. What he believed was that his value to his father was in how he could make his father look to his father's peers.

When children are treated as peers with no parent/child distinction, they will feel abandoned by their parents. Many times parents develop relationships with their children in which they are their friends, their peers, their equals. In doing so, they share information that is not age-appropriate for a child. Inappropriate information often creates a sense of burden, or even guilt, for children, and that is not fair. To tell a ten-year-old daughter that her father has had an affair cannot offer the daughter any security. The mother may need to talk about it, but that needs to be with someone who has the adult resources to be able to offer appropriate support or feedback. To share with an eight-year-old son the fears related to a situation at work only makes the child feel that his parent needs support and is too vulnerable to be available as a source of protection.

<u>Abandonment</u> **plus** <u>distorted boundaries</u> **at a time when children are developing their sense of worth is the foundation to the belief in their own inadequacy, and the central cause of their shame.** When parents are disrespectful of their children's boundaries and violate them, the message given is that they don't value a child as a person. That message becomes internalized as "I am not of value. I am not worthy." When parents don't acknowledge children's boundaries, the message they give is "You are here to meet my needs,"

and/or "I am more important than you," and/or "It is not okay to be your own person with individual feelings, desires, or needs." The message also implies that the children have to give up themselves to be available to another. This internalizes to the belief, "I am bad for having different, or separate, needs, wants, and feelings." "I, in my uniqueness, am not of value." When children experience chronic abandonment with distorted boundaries, they live in fear and doubt about their worth.

The greater the clarity a child has around boundaries, understanding who is responsible for what, and the greater a child's self-esteem, the more likely a child will be able to reject, rather than internalize, shameful behaviors and messages. The following is an example of a young person, Sandi, who, in spite of the fact that she was raised in an alcoholic family, experienced some stability in her early years. As a result, she developed a sense of self and self-esteem which helped her ward off shame. "Up until I was about eight, home seemed okay. I felt valued, life was fun. Then as if it was overnight, my dad was always angry. My mom was preoccupied and distant or very sad. It was as if neither of our parents had any time for us. Looking back now I realized that something was happening. I just couldn't figure it out . No one was talking about what was wrong. Life just became more and frightening. I tried to not get in the way. I took care of my brother and sister. I tried to do things to make my dad and mom happy. Nothing I did really made a difference."

Because Sandi had experienced security and safety in her very early years though, she developed a sense of self-worth and a degree of autonomy that helped prevent her from taking on shame. One night when she was sixteen and cheerleading at a basketball game, her father showed up so drunk he could hardly walk on his own and created a scene that nearly incited a racial riot. With her father's arms thrown over her shoulders and her pom poms tucked under her arms, Sandi was leading her drunk father out of the gym when he began to scream racial slurs at a group of African-American teenagers. "He said things I never heard him or any one else say," Sandi said. "He said things I never knew he thought. Thank heaven this group of kids couldn't reach us. It was all I could do to get him out of the gym. Everyone was screaming and jeering. Well, I got him into his friend's car and off they went. I didn't know why my dad acted like he did—I was so angry at him."

Sandi had the ability to be angry because she had not previously internalized shame and therefore could clearly differentiate who was responsible for what. She had healthy boundary distinctions. She knew what took place in the gym was about her father, not her. Because she did not take this incident as a statement about her worth or value, she was also able to access other feelings. With shame, we lose the ability to identify our feelings and we are more likely to reinstate the Don't Talk rule. Sandi said she was angry, and then became sad. She could talk about her fear. While this scene was certainly an act of abandonment by her father, she nonetheless had an emotional boundary that protected her self-worth and her autonomy.

Sandi's ability to maintain a healthy emotional boundary ("My father's behavior does not determine who I am") which prevented her from feeling shamed and personally diminished by her father's behavior requires the same kind of skills necessary to ward off shame in a less public situation. Linda was born into an already hectic, frightened family. Her first memories were of hiding behind a table in the kitchen, trying not to be noticed, while listening to her parents arguing and thinking to herself, "Just don't let them see me." She spent most of her life trying to be invisible. "In my family there was a lot of arguing, unhappiness, and a lot of moving from place to place. I was the youngest of four and an unplanned pregnancy. My mother let me know right away she was content with three babies, not four. I felt I came out of the shoot needing a protective shield, trying to ward off the hurtful words, the painful glares. I was always in their way. Yet I worked so hard not to be. My very existence seemed like such a thorn." When childhood is like Linda's, spent on survival, there is little energy left to develop a separate sense of self, an autonomous self. Linda was chronically abandoned, subject to emotional boundary abuse, and as a result, experienced and internalized shame.

When we are, in essence, abandoned by our caretakers, we will not perceive that they were bad people or what they did to us was bad. Children cannot reject bad parents because parents are needed so desperately. Children always feel that a bad object is better than no object at all. Instead, they will internalize that they are bad themselves. In other words, children take the burden of badness on themselves. In doing this, they purge their caretakers of badness, which reinforces a sense of security. It is well recognized that mistreated children who cope with intolerable environments are, in fact, very apt to project goodness onto their parents and badness onto themselves. In effect, outer safety is purchased at the price of inner security.

Abandonment, plus distorted or undefined boundaries as you are developing your worth and identity, creates shame and fear. This truth bears repeating because it defines the root of our pain. What we must understand now is that our abandonment experiences and boundary violations were in no way indictments of our innate goodness and value. Instead, they revealed the flawed thinking, false beliefs, and impaired behaviors of those who hurt us. Still, the wounds were struck deep in our young hearts and minds, and the very real pain can still be felt today. The causes of our emotional injury need to be understood and accepted so we can heal. Until we do, the pain will stay with us, becoming a driving force in our adult lives.

PAST-DRIVEN, PRESENT PAIN

In recovery we seek to change the course in our present lives by healing the pain of our past. That means we also must address the pain that results from our past-driven, present-day beliefs and behaviors. As a result of the pain of our past experiences, we adopted false beliefs, i.e., "I can't make a mistake or I will be worthless," or "I have to produce to be of value." We learned defense skills, i.e., to blame others before they blame us. We developed cognitive defense mechanisms, i.e., to deny, minimize, or rationalize. We developed mechanisms to distract us from our pain, i.e., excessive behaviors, or we found ways to literally numb our pain, i.e., food or alcohol and other drugs. All of these are strategies for the preservation of ourselves when our Self is threatened.

Jan said, "I knew my parents loved me. They provided for me. They came to my school events. They told me they loved me. They would hug me. Yet, they would blatantly reject me if I showed feelings of sadness or anger. There was clearly a Don't Talk rule around being emotional unless the feelings were positive. My shame was for having feelings. So while I knew I was valued in one way, I felt very rejected and abandoned in other ways. There was a lot of loss in my family. My dad lost his job and did not find one for four years. My mother had to be hospitalized for unknown reasons twice when I was between nine and eleven. My sister went to live with my grandmother during those times. And we weren't to talk about any of this. I was angry. I was very frightened. I was sad. I wanted to scream so I could be heard, and yet knew I would not be heard and only banished further."

Jan did what most of us do when feeling abandonment and fear— she did her best to be "lovable" so her family would be there for her. Being lovable would be defined by others. For Jan, it meant discounting her own feelings and needs and putting those of others ahead of hers, which in turn meant distancing from herself. Jan learned these defenses and skills as a young girl, and now these are the only defenses and skills she knows for protecting herself and relating to others. Paradoxically, Jan's beliefs and behaviors do not protect her now, but actually cause her more pain. Unfortunately, these will continue throughout her adult life until the painful weight of chronically discounting her needs and feelings is so great that she is no longer able to continue as she has. Then she will seek new, different protectors, often harmful ways, such as alcohol or prescription pills. These present-day protections will only perpetuate, and probably escalate, her pain until she turns from the course of protecting from pain to the path of healing her pain.

Most people develop protective strategies when they are young, carrying them into adulthood with slight, age-related differences. For example, as a child you may have used food to medicate your pain, and continue to use food this way as an adult, but now also use alcohol as a medication. Or, as a child, if you used people-pleasing behaviors to get attention from parents, you may also employ this strategy to get attention in the work place.

The mechanisms we develop to reduce our anxiety and fears are defensive protectors. *In no way should we ever be critical of what we needed to do to protect ourselves growing up.* Today, though, we need to recognize when these defenses and protectors are intrusive in our lives, or when they create more harm and pain. The purpose or theme of these strategies has been to lessen the perception or feeling of abandonment; also to compartmentalize or distance ourselves from the incredible fear and sense of powerlessness. The basis for all these attempts is to control or compensate for the pain.

The burden of pain we presently carry and try so hard to control is the combination of unresolved pain from the past *plus* pain from the present. As we know, events and family conditions that caused our past pain cannot be changed, but our response to pain is a choice we are making in the present. And how we choose to respond can change the course of our lives. Our pain, our choice of responses, and the consequences of our choices are summarized on the following chart, "Pain From An Adult's Point Of View." In the next pages, we'll discuss how people respond to pain so we will be able to understand the choices we can make.

ATTEMPTS TO CONTROL OUR PAIN

Whether or not we understood the source of our pain in our early lives, we felt it. We were anxious, fearful, saddened, or angry. To live with a high degree of emotional pain was so unbearable for most of us that we sought ways to control the pain to defend against it. Ironically and unfortunately, as we have now seen, these ways created their own pain.

As adults still trying to control our pain, we have sought ways to create a sense of control or power, to compensate for the overwhelming experience of powerlessness. We have attempted to control the pain and/or to control the sources of pain. We have tried to be in control to protect ourselves from further exposure, so that our vul-

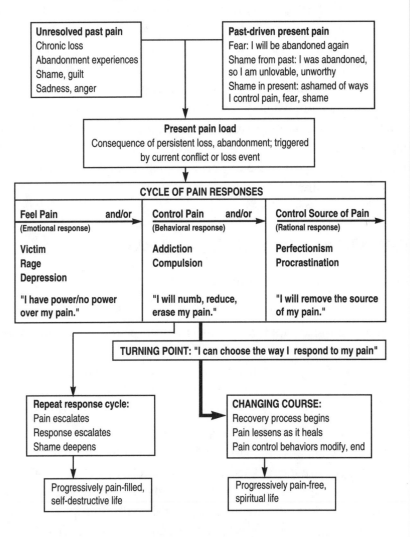

From A Past Of Chronic Loss To The Turning Point
Pain from an Adult's Point of View

Unresolved past pain
Chronic loss
Abandonment experiences
Shame, guilt
Sadness, anger

Past-driven present pain
Fear: I will be abandoned again
Shame from past: I was abandoned,
so I am unlovable, unworthy
Shame in present: ashamed of ways
I control pain, fear, shame

Present pain load
Consequence of persistent loss, abandonment; triggered
by current conflict or loss event

CYCLE OF PAIN RESPONSES

Feel Pain and/or
(Emotional response)

Victim
Rage
Depression

"I have power/no power
over my pain."

Control Pain and/or
(Behavioral response)

Addiction
Compulsion

"I will numb, reduce,
erase my pain."

Control Source of Pain
(Rational response)

Perfectionism
Procrastination

"I will remove the source
of my pain."

TURNING POINT: "I can choose the way I respond to my pain"

Repeat response cycle:
Pain escalates
Response escalates
Shame deepens

CHANGING COURSE:
Recovery process begins
Pain lessens as it heals
Pain control behaviors modify, end

Progressively pain-filled,
self-destructive life

Progressively pain-free,
spiritual life

Causes of past pain cannot be changed.
Responses to pain, both past and present, can change.
Changing responses to pain changes the course of
pain in life.

nerability would not be visible. We have tried to be in control so that no one would ever shame us again and so that we would not have to feel our pain.

We feel our pain. We medicate our pain. We rationalize our pain. These are all responses to the pain we have felt for so long. Then we have responded to our feeling powerless over the pain, or powerless to be able to impact our own lives in a way that creates a difference.

We first respond to pain on an emotional level, most commonly in terms of victimization, rage, and depression. Then, in an attempt to control the pain, we may respond with behaviors that try to medicate it with alcohol, drugs, foods, or compulsive behaviors. Last, we may respond on a rational level, thinking we can avoid the pain if we don't do anything to cause it. Perfectionism and procrastination are two cognitive attempts to control pain by avoiding it.

EMOTIONAL RESPONSES TO PAIN

Victimization As A Response To Pain

Chronic victimization, that is, chronically assuming the role of the victim, is the result when we accept and operate on the shameful messages that we internalized as a result of the abandonment. It is a combination of not believing in our own worth, and not developing the skills that go with a belief in our worthiness, such as setting limits. When we have internalized beliefs, such as "I am not worthy," "I am not of value," "Other people are more important than me," or "Other people are more worthy," then it is difficult to set limits. We don't believe we have the right to set limits. We do not know how to say no. Those of us who are victims struggle with appropriate boundaries. We are most apt not to have boundaries or boundaries that are easily permeable.

Victims have learned not to trust their own perceptions, believing that another person's perception is accurate instead of theirs. They always give others the benefit of the doubt and are willing to respond to the structure others set. Victims are not apt to question.

After all, they believe "Who am I to question?"

Not believing in their own worth, victims often fail to realize they even have needs and, as a result, do not take care of themselves. They operate from a position of fear, unable to access any anger or indignation that comes with being hurt, or disappointed, or even abused. When asked what they need or want, victims often do not know.

While the development of the victim response is enveloped by the deepest belief in personal powerlessness, it is clearly a response to the intense emotional pain in one's life. It not only is an outcome of helplessness, it is also a kind of defense in that victims believe they may be not have as much pain if they give in, or abdicate their autonomy, to another.

Victims have developed a high tolerance for pain and for inappropriate behavior. They have become emotionally separated from themselves by becoming highly skilled at rationalizing, minimizing, and often flatly denying the events and emotions in their lives. They are not as readily able to identify others' behavior that has hurt them because that would, in their perception, create a greater feeling of helplessness or invite more trouble.

Some victims stay in isolation. Those who choose to stay more visible often play a victim/martyr situation: "Look at how I am victimized! Aren't they terrible for doing this to me! I will just have to endure." Being victim becomes part of a cycle. Victims already feel bad about themselves as a result of being abandoned and/or used and abused. Then they don't act in a way that provides safety and security for themselves, leading to greater abandonment, use or abuse.

Typically, the greater a person's shame, the more likely he or she will invite someone else with tremendous shame into their lives. Very often, for the victim, this other person is someone who appears to have the ability to take charge, make things happen, someone who feels strength by association with the victim's vulnerability. Depending on the specific history of the two people involved, that attraction often leads to the dominant one battering the victim, either emotionally or physically.

Almost inevitably, victims have great difficulty protecting themselves in the context of intimate relationships. For example, a woman may have such a desperate longing for nurturance and care that it makes it difficult for her to establish safe and appropriate boundaries with others. Her tendency to denigrate herself and to idealize those to whom she becomes attached further clouds her judgment. In this case, her empathic attunement to the wishes of others and her automatic, often unconscious habits of obedience also make her vulnerable to anyone in a position of power or authority. Her defensive style makes it difficult for her to form conscious and accurate assessments of danger.

For all of the reasons noted above, whether male or female, the shameful person is at great risk of repeated victimization.

Rage As Response To Pain

Rage is the holding tank for accumulated fears, angers, humiliations, and shame. It is an honest response to no longer wanting to endure the pain. Emotionally, rage is an attempt to be heard, seen, and valued when people are most desperate and lacking in other resources. For some people rage becomes integrated into their lifestyle. Growing up, they found anger to be the one safe feeling for them to express, so all their other vulnerabilities were masked with anger. Many people who are rageful don't show any sign of emotions, keeping a tight lid on all of their feelings until something triggers an eruption. There may not be signs of any feeling, and suddenly their rage is in someone else's face; a scathing memo at work; an outburst of criticism at service providers, i.e., waiters, gas station attendants, etc.; a lack of tolerance for any disagreement in a discussion, followed by a theatrical exit; or a lashing out verbally or physically.

While people with chronic rage do exist, they are not tolerated in most neighborhoods or communities and usually live isolated with someone who is often the chronic victim of their rage; or they move around a lot, wearing out their welcome after relatively short periods of time in one place. While we may view others' rage as being out of control, those who are ragers feel very much in control and powerful. They no longer feel inadequate and defective. Rage is intended to protect against further experiences of pain. Rage is a way of actively compensating for powerlessness and feelings of shame by offering a false, but attractive (to the rager) sense of power. When rage is the only way people know to protect against their emptiness, their powerlessness, and their pain, their choice is a quick one. Rage also offers protection in that rageful behavior keeps people at a distance. As a result, other people cannot see into the raging person's inner self that he or she believes to be so ugly.

Rage as a defense offers protection not only by keeping others away, but also by transferring the shame to them. The outwardly rageful person chooses a victim-like person who, consciously or not, is willing to take the abuse and take on or assume the shame. Rage can be accumulated anger that has never seemed safe to expose.

When anger is not safe, it becomes internalized, and with time it grows, festering into chronic bitterness, or even more likely, chronic depression, as we will discuss next. When there has been no outlet for rage, it is more apt to explode suddenly as a significant single hostile act such as physical abuse, even a murder. Such an act is the consequence of the accumulation of feelings without the skills to tolerate painful feelings, to resolve conflict, or to perceive options and choices.

Depression As A Response To Pain

Unfortunately, a depressed person is typically pictured as one who sleeps excessively, maybe eighteen hours per day, is unable to eat, and is suicidal. While that picture represents the severe end of the depression continuum, most adults from troubled families who are depressed are able to function daily, meeting their required responsibilities. After all, that has been their survival mode. When feelings cannot be expressed and so a person's emotions must necessarily be shut down, this naturally leads to depression. The false self that adult survivors present to the world may not have the look of depression, but their true self, their mental and emotional self, is experiencing great despair. "Looking good" children, as described in *It Will Never Happen To Me*, maintain the outward appearance of "doing just fine while dying on the inside." These are people who, like an addicted person, manipulate life so their true self cannot be seen. They are what I call "closeted depressed."

To keep depression hidden, those of us who are depressed avoid getting close enough or spending enough time around others who may recognize our true feelings and the pervasive emptiness our depression is masking. Nor do we develop close friendships where others are invested enough to "pull our covers." We appear very capable and seem to put out an impenetrable force field that says, "Don't ask me about me. Don't push me." It is difficult enough being depressed. It is even more difficult when we have shame around it— shame as one cause of depression, added shame because we are depressed.

There are many different theories about the cause of depression. Some clinicians and researchers believe it to be a biochemical imbalance, a disordered neurochemistry, best treated with antidepressants. It is commonly accepted among professionals that depression tends to run in families, suggesting there may be a physiological predisposition towards depression. Yet, many other theories support the belief that depression is a consequence of a habitually pessimistic and disordered way of viewing the world and is a consequence of loss and the inability to do the griefwork necessary to bring completion to the feelings of sorrow. [Note: All depression needs to be assessed by a qualified physician.]

There is tremendous loss associated with being raised in a shame-based family. With the family being denial-centered, as it often is, and it not being okay to talk honestly, the sense of loss is amplified because there is no way to work through the pain. The hurt, the disappointment, the fears, and the angers associated with life events as well as with abandonment experiences are all swirled together and internalized. When you add to this a personal belief that says you are at fault, it is easy to see why you came to believe that you are not worthy, and so try to hide your real self from others. Also, you can see that eventually, whether you are thirty-five or fifty-five, suddenly you hit a wall. The burden of hiding eventually becomes too heavy, and all of those protecting, controlling mechanisms that kept you going for so long just stop working. The depression is there. Most people who experience depression related to loss are extremely frightened of their feelings. And they have so much to feel about. When it is not safe to speak these feelings, they become directed inward against the self. This becomes another means of perpetuating shame, which then further protracts the depressive mood.

As discussed in chapter 1, there are necessary and unnecessary losses in life. Because it was not safe to acknowledge them, we didn't learn coping skills for the loss that would occur in our adult years. So, when loss occurs and/or accumulates in adulthood, we resort to the same defenses we have always used to deny what we are feeling.

When we have incredible grief and loss in our lives, many of us develop thought processes wherein we catastrophize and exaggerate fear to such a point that we feel hopeless and in despair. For example, when your husband is twenty minutes late for an important appointment, you think he must have been in a terrible car accident. When your boss forgot to say hello, you feel certain that she is angry with you and is going to let you go. Given some small bit of knowledge, we presume the worst will happen.

Over the years, given our experiences, we have developed a committee of internal voices that have become our Inner Critic, telling ourselves we are stupid, not wanted, ugly, and not important, in response to any slight or perceived loss, or when not being fully embraced by someone we value.

Most adults from troubled families experience a combination of both—unresolved loss and a pessimistic view of life. When we feel our powerlessness, our despair, and our fear, we send ourselves into a downhill spiral so quickly anybody's head would be spinning.

Acute Episodes Of Depression

Many adults make their way through life cut off from their internal pain, until they experience an important present-day loss—the last child leaving home, a significant health problem, the death of a close friend or family member, the loss of job or career opportunity. As great numbers of women enter perimenopausal and menopausal stages, the combination of physical changes and the symbolism around such changes can create an incredible sense of loss. For men and women both, one significant present loss can be the straw that breaks the camel's back. In other words, that current loss can trigger the beginning of a downward emotional spiral in which the adult becomes overwhelmed in despair, shame, powerlessness, and depression.

Sally, who was raised in a physically abusive home, was a department manager in an engineering firm. She had tucked away the pain of her childhood history into a corner of her heart and put a lock on it. She was involved in raising her own family, and kept a distant relationship with her sister and parents. All aspects of her life were compartmentalized. Then one day, she lost her oldest daughter in an accident, and six months after that, her father died. Three weeks later, Sally made her first suicide attempt. To lose a child is one of life's greatest tragedies for anybody. Further, Sally had no skills, no internal supports to deal with the intense pain when her daughter died. While she did not feel close to her father, his death unleashed all of the childhood pain she had so neatly and quietly tucked away. When present-day loss occurs, we may not be aware of remembering our growing-up years, but we are certainly feeling the accumulated pain.

Tom, who was raised in an extremely critical home and felt his loss through chronic rejection, quickly separated from his parents and all his siblings after high school. Then, at the age of twenty-eight when his fiancée broke up with him, his exaggerated and catastrophic thinking led into incredible despair. He had talked himself into seeing himself as totally unworthy. He envisioned that his fiancée would marry someone much more financially stable than he was and certainly a lot more fun and exciting. She would have children with someone else. He would be alone all of his life. He was convinced he would never find happiness. He would never be able to offer anything to anyone else anyway. On and on and on Tom's incredibly painful thinking continued. Soon, he was sleeping twelve to fourteen hours a day, missing days at work, and no longer exercising or eating properly.

Losing a relationship, particularly in young adulthood, happens to many of us. However, because of chronic losses in his childhood, Tom had not learned the skills needed to grieve through the loss of his fiancée. He was not able to understand the experience in any way except as further evidence of his inadequacy and worthlessness. This loss was simply one more that added fuel to his already existing fire of shame.

Like victimization, depression is a consequence of the inability to defend and protect ourselves against the pain of loss.

Suicide: The Most Severe Response To Pain

"I am hopeless. I am unworthy and I don't deserve to live. Life won't get any better and I can't stand this pain." Suicidal thoughts, attempts, and completions speak of many issues. They are often a reflection of anger and rage turned inward and of depression.

For some people, the act of suicide seems to claim power to compensate for their powerlessness in life. For others, death is perceived to be a better option than to live with certain memories and shame. The pain is too overwhelming, and out of despair and hopelessness, people become their own victims. Thoughts of taking our own lives are much more prevalent than people realize. While pain creates such thoughts, we also experience shame for having the thoughts. My message to you is, Please don't feel ashamed. But, please do speak up and let someone know how frightened, angry, or hopeless you are feeling.

In recovery, you CAN speak about those issues that have created the pain. You CAN say NO to your shame. You CAN learn to find ways to express your anger without hurting yourself. You CAN develop new beliefs and behaviors that support you in the way you deserve to be supported. You CAN learn how to access the power within you that does exist. You deserve to be able to live without pain. But when you are considering suicide as a way out of your pain, you must reach out and get assistance from a helping professional.

BEHAVIORAL RESPONSES TO PAIN

"Medicating" Pain

Along with the ways we feel our past and past-driven present pain, whether our emotional response is one of victimization, rage, or depression, we may also try different behaviors to control our pain, hoping to lessen the hurt. Unfortunately, our efforts to control the pain don't remove the cause or source of our feeling. One way people try to control and regulate their pain is by "medicating" it through addiction to substances or compulsive behaviors.

Addictions

Types of addictions may range from chemical dependency to food, to caffeine, nicotine, sugar, alcohol, and other drugs. Many of the substances people become addicted to are socially sanctioned and supported, making it very difficult for those abusing them to see how they are using them in unhealthy ways. [Note: In terms of ending specific addictions, in nearly all cases abstinence is the goal. Also, it is vital to recognize that once someone is addicted, willpower or self-control is no longer a relevant issue.]

In addition to temporarily controlling our pain, the substances we use and abuse very often provide something for us we do not know how to seek naturally. As an example, alcohol may give a sense of power to someone who has only known powerlessness. It may give access to a sense of courage and confidence to someone who feels lacking. This is certainly drug-induced and false, but for many people, false is better than none. For someone who is isolated and feels alienated from others, alcohol makes it easier to reach out to people. "Give me a little bit to drink and I become alive. I pull myself away from the wall and I find myself talking, laughing, listening. I see people responding to me and I like it." This kind of thinking doesn't mean that a person is addicted, but it does mean he or she is thirsty for connection with others. This person has expressed a need for psychological reinforcement in order to feel whole and complete.

For people who have never taken time for play or laughter because life has been so serious and "I have to get things done," alcohol gives them the opportunity to relax. Alice identified, "My entire life has been spent taking care of other people. I am always busy. I make these lists daily, thinking the world will stop if I don't get the job done. I don't think about missing out on fun—it has never been a part of my life.

"I was a teetotaler. I never drank until I was twenty-six. I don't even know why I started. But those first few times I remember thinking that I was being silly, hearing myself laugh with other people. It actually scared me. Yet, at the same time there was this attraction. It was as if there was this whole other part of me I didn't know and maybe was okay to know.

"The attraction to relaxing with alcohol kept getting stronger. I can actually remember thinking, 'I don't have to make this decision tonight,' or 'I don't have to do this by myself.' Pretty soon it was, 'I don't have to do this at all.' I was having fun. I was relaxing." While Alice's new ways of letting go and becoming less rigid were not harmful, because she did not know how to do it without alcohol, she ultimately became dependent on it. Alice, like so many others, was seeking wholeness. But the only glimpse she had of it was "under the influence."

Variations of this scenario fit for other addictions. Our relationship to certain foods or the intake, lack of intake, and/or purging of food may be about an internal struggle with power and control. We may be attempting to access power that we don't have the skills or confidence to access more naturally. Starving ourselves, purging, and compulsive overeating may be anger turned toward ourselves. Possibly we are punishing ourselves for being bad. The anorexic may be literally starving herself to become invisible in response to shame; the anorexic and bulimic may be seeking perfection — which is based in shame.

When we come from a pain-based family, it is common to go outside of ourselves for a quick answer to relieve our suffering. It doesn't seem possible that we have any way to help ourselves. Yet, ultimately, we can keep our pain under control only so long before it starts to leak out. Frightened, we feel out of control and we seek a medicator. Sometimes that medicator is a person; it could possibly be an activity; many times it is a substance. Often it is a combination of compulsions and addictions.

Compulsions

To experience shame and powerlessness is to be in intolerable pain. While physical pain is horrible, there are moments of relief. There is hope of being cured. However, with shame, when we believe we are defective, there is no cure; shame is a defeated state. We have no relationship with ourselves or anyone else; we are totally alone. Relief from this intolerable pain must come, one way or another. We need someone or something to take away our profound loneliness and fear, and so we assume we need a mood-altering experience. We need an escape. Everyone has certain behaviors used as a way to "escape," but it is when we come to depend on them to relieve our unworthiness that these become compulsive in nature. And when we grow up in an environment of shaming, where the cause of pain is external, we develop the belief that the solutions to problems exist only externally, i.e., substances or behaviors that are medicators.

There are many different types of addictions and compulsions ranging from compulsively repeated activities, to preoccupying thoughts, to relationship dependencies. We use some form of keeping busy to distance or to distract ourselves, to get our minds off our pain, our fear, or our anger. We keep busy to stay in control of our feelings and therefore to avoid feeling bad. Many behavioral compulsions would be otherwise harmless activities if they weren't exaggerated, destroying the balance in our lives. For example, exercise is a healthy activity until done so excessively that we actually injure our bodies.

Relationship addiction is the dependence on being in a relationship to provide our worth. That means we use other people to lessen our shame and to avoid truly facing our selves.

Sex addiction is the use of sexual stimulation to act as a detractor or medicator of pain; or it may be a false way of accessing power to overcome our sense of powerlessness. Compulsive sex experiences can temporarily offer us warmth and an appearance of love. Or we can act out sex as an expression of anger. These sex experiences may temporarily affirm that we are lovable and worthy, all the while compounding our belief in our defectiveness. Sex addicts vary in their focus, from obsessive masturbating, using pornographic materials, exhibitionism, obscene phone calls, voyeurism, multiple affairs, and so on. For sex addicts, certain behaviors take on sexual meaning; they view objects and people through their preoccupation.

Even though compulsive behaviors distract and alter feelings, feelings themselves can become compulsive in nature. We become dependent on certain feelings to mask and avoid experiencing what we are really feeling. We may become a rageaholic, using rage as a release for all feelings. Fear can overwhelm us, where phobias, hypervigilance, and/or anxieties can control our lives.

While some compulsions are certainly more harmful to ourselves and our family, others may be considered only nuisances. Substances and behaviors can detract from, medicate and/or anesthetize, and, therefore, attempt to control whether or not we feel our pain. Yet, any time we use a substance or become involved in a process or behavior that interferes with our honesty, our ability to be present with ourselves, it deserves our attention.

RATIONAL OR COGNITIVE RESPONSES TO PAIN

While some people focus on controlling the pain itself, others attempt to control the source of the pain. Control is the key word here. These people hope to control the cause of the pain, as opposed to removing, releasing, or healing it. As with the emotional and behavioral responses discussed earlier, these cognitive or rational responses try to prevent potential abandonment and prevent the possibility of exposing their shameful selves.

Perfectionism
Our common rational or cognitive response to pain is perfectionism. Perfectionism is driven by the belief that if a person's behavior is perfect, there will be no reason to be criticized and therefore no more cause for pain. However, perfectionism is a shame-based phenomenon because children learn that "no matter what they do, it's never good enough." As a result, in their struggle to feel good about themselves and relieve the source of pain, they constantly push to excel, to be the best.

Highly perfectionistic people are usually people who have been raised in a rigid family environment. The rigidity may be in the form of unrealistic expectations that parents have for their children and/or for themselves. Either way, the parents' expectations are internalized by the children. Also, rigidity may be expressed as children feel the need to do things "right" in order to get approval from their parents and to lessen fears of rejection. For most children, being "right" is perceived to mean there was no room for mistakes.

Let's look at the example of Teri, nineteen years old, in a therapy group and talking about being a perfectionist. When she was in junior high school, she related, in order to be able to visit with friends on Saturday afternoon, she had to complete certain household tasks. So, every Saturday morning she would approach her father to get a list of what she needed to accomplish to be able to go out later in the day. She'd get her typewritten list and go on about her duties. When the list was completed, she'd return it to her father, but at this point, he'd give her a second list. When she was done with that list, he inevitably gave her a third list. Often times a fourth and fifth list.

As you can guess, Teri didn't spend a lot of Saturday afternoons with her friends. When Teri told this story, tears streamed down her cheeks. Then she paused and reflectively commented, "But we all come from some pretty crazy families. It could have been worse. Besides I learned a few things. If you want something done, ask me. I know how to be quick." Then haltingly she added, "What I really learned was that no matter what I do, it's never good enough."

That was the lesson for Teri. No matter what she did, it wasn't good enough. But what Teri did need to learn is that whether or not she was permitted to spend time with her friends was not about how well or how quick she was in her work. Nothing was good enough, because it wasn't humanly possible to please her father. This Saturday ritual was not about Teri. It was about her father and his need to control, his need for power. Ultimately, for her own well-being, Teri needed to acknowledge that. In doing so, she would be able to establish an emotional boundary, separating her worth from her father's criticism.

Unfortunately, most perfectionists have no internal sense of limits. With shame and fear nipping at their heels the entire time, they always perceive their performance as related to a standard or judgment outside themselves. As children, they were taught to strive onward. There was never a time or place to rest or to have inner joy and satisfaction.

Perfection as a performance criteria means you never measure up. Then, not measuring up is translated into a comparison with others of good versus bad, better versus worse. Inevitably you end up feeling the lesser for the comparison. Comparison with others is one of the primary ways that people continue to create more shame for themselves. You continue to do to yourself on the inside what was done to you from the outside. Since your efforts were never experienced as sufficient, adequate, or good enough, you did not develop an internal sense of how much is good enough.

As adults, we need to identify those areas where we once strived so hard for recognition, attention, and approval. Then we need to recognize that not only did we do our best, we truly were good enough. The lack of acceptance we have felt is not about us or our worth, but about those who judged us and who also sought to feel a sense of power by threatening to reject us. While we were not able to understand that as children, we can come to terms with that today.

Procrastination And Ambivalence

Procrastination, such as starting but not completing a project, or considering a project but never initiating it, is often an attempt to defend against further shame. Perfectionism and procrastination are closely linked. It is easy to picture Teri, in the above example, never finishing her first list, realizing that she could not please her father. Teri, though, believed in herself a bit more strongly than most people who procrastinate. Often, the procrastinator has little confidence and more fear. The perfectionist is more apt to follow through because there is the possibility of the reinforcement of some sense of accomplishment. The procrastinator will not even see that possibility.

Some children received so little attention that they were not encouraged to initiate projects, let alone to complete them. Too many times when these children did something, drew a picture or wrote a story, and gleefully showed their parents, the parents barely looked at it and then set it aside, or maybe even lost it. When there is no positive reinforcement to complete school projects or homework, children perform with ambivalence. They believe that "No one else cares," and develop the attitude, "Why should I care?" The result is procrastination and ambivalence.

It was just as painful for children when their parents did pay attention, but were constantly critical, maybe making a joke of the children's work, possibly humiliating them in front of others. Sue, who was an average student in school, became very excited about a history project during her sophomore year of high school. "I worked hard on it all quarter, which was unusual for me, but I found this real interesting and the teacher liked me, so I really wanted to do well.

One night I was at the dining room table putting all of the pages of my report in a notebook to be turned in the next day in class. I wasn't expecting my parents to come home for a few hours yet, so I was shocked when my mother and stepfather came in, both laughing loudly, both drunk. Mom asked what I was doing and then picked up my paper which was titled, Did America Need To Be In World War II? Suddenly, she was in a rage and calling me a communist, saying I wasn't patriotic.

"It was unreal. Within minutes, they were both screaming at me calling me all kinds of names. They took my report and, in their words, threw the 'trash' into the fireplace. Well, there was no way I could tell the teacher what had happened. I just took a failing grade. It was pretty horrifying, but I should have known not to put that much effort into anything. Most things never worked out for me too much."

Sue's sense of defeat was a culmination of similar experiences. Whenever she put forth effort to achieve, she somehow always felt diminished. It was several years before she could put into perspective the report incident and all the smaller incidents that led her to believe even if she wanted to work at something, it probably wasn't worth the effort. As a result, Sue quit trying to achieve at a very young age.

When children are humiliated for their efforts, made to feel inadequate or stupid, they find ways to protect themselves so they can't do something that would prove they really are a failure.

In addition, children become discouraged when they are constantly compared to someone who "did it better" or might have done it better. Tom says he was always compared to his two older brothers. "My two older brothers were articulate. They were quick and did well in school. It took me longer to grasp things. I wasn't as interested in math and sciences as they were. I was more interested in my friends. So, with school being more of a struggle and having no real help from my parents, only the push that 'You should be like your brothers,' I just gave up. I wasn't like them and didn't feel I could be."

Also mixed into procrastination can be anger, expressed as an attitude of "I'll show you—I won't finish this," or "I'll only do it part way. I won't give my best." Inherent in this attitude is a challenge that insists, "Like me for who I am, not for what I do." In a family where rigidity is the rule, where it is not okay to make mistakes, not okay to take risks or be different, not okay to draw attention to yourself, you learn not to initiate, or not to finish what you started. For those of us raised this way, it is amazing that we get anything done.

Understanding Your Defenses Against Pain

Rage, depression, victimization, addictions, compulsions, perfectionism, and procrastination—these are some of the responses, which are results of having lived with fear and pain. They often became protectors. They offered to control the pain itself and/or control the source of the pain. Other protectors begin as common, everyday acts, but taken to extremes create negative outcomes in the long run. Some of these are intellectualization, physical isolation, humor, magical thinking, lying, silence, and withdrawal.

What are the defenses you employ? It would be helpful for you to make a list of defenses you developed to defend against the pain. Are those still behaviors you use today? After you make your list, then ask yourself the following questions:

- What did it [the protective behavior] do for you in the past?

- What is it doing for you now?

- Would you like to let go of it?

- What do you need to do to let it go?

- What is interfering with your ability to let go of it?

LETTING GO OF THE PAST, HEALING THE PAIN

Every one of us would like to rid ourselves of pain. The answer lies in being willing to admit and show your pain. That means facing the feelings. It means being willing to own the sadness, the hurt and the fears, embarrassments and anger about how you have had to live your life. It means being willing to be specific about all the ways you fought for emotional survivorship, how you attempted to compensate for powerlessness, how you tried to gain control, to overcome the incredible sense of shame and fear that have been so significant in your life, in the past and the past-driven present.

LOSS EXPERIENCES AS ADULTS

Creating A Loss Graph For Your Adult Years

Ultimately, you will need to identify the loss events, conditions, and shaming messages in your adult life, as well as those in your growing up years, in order to be able to become separate from them. An adult loss graph, like the loss graph of your early years, is a very useful way to begin to identify the difference between who you are and what has happened to you.

To create a loss graph for your adult years, you will need to record the loss events you experienced as an adult, your age at the time, and the feelings that you remember having when the losses occurred. Also, you need to record loss conditions and abandonment experiences and feelings that have been a part of your adult life. When you create this loss graph, remember that you are trying to record your adult experiences—not those you remember having happened when you were a child.

Loss conditions, however, are different from loss events and abandonment experiences. A condition is a state that exists over time, so adult loss conditions may very likely include unresolved childhood conditions. If your childhood losses are still creating pain for you in the present, then this is a very real condition in your adult life. To illustrate adult loss graphs, the following examples have been created, once again for "Joyce" and "Tim." In the appendix, there is a blank graph form for you to record the losses in your adult years.

Loss Graph For Adult Years

Joyce

Loss Events:	Miscarriage	Divorce	Left college prematurely due to stress	Aware of marital infidelity	Loses job promotion
Age:	21	23	24	36	38
Unattended Feelings:	Despair	Despair fear	Sad	Anger frightened insecure	Despair

Loss conditions in Family:	Unresolved childhood pain; Emotionally abusive partner; Compulsive overeater.	Abandonment Experiences/Feelings:	Inadequate; frightened; sad; ashamed; anger.

Joyce carried into adulthood the unresolved feelings of her childhood. Added to this, was the pain of adult loss events, pain which she had not yet learned to work through. The feelings were there, but she was unable to attend to them. In addition, she chose a partner that fueled her sense of shame and abandonment. Her compulsive overeating only heightened the accumulation of these feelings. Except for her compulsive overeating, most people saw Joyce as a happily married mother of two daughters, who worked as a medical records specialist in a community hospital. Joyce's loss graph, however, offers a strong, visual record of pain, a striking contrast to her public image.

Loss Graph For Adult Years Tim

Loss Events:	Engagement broken	Loses job	Son, 6 years old, diagnosed w/ cancer
Age:	24	26	36
Unattended Feelings:	Angry sad	Angry frightened	Frightened sad
Loss Conditions in Family:	Unresoved childhood and Vietnam pain; Wife depressed; Chronic conflict around child's loss of health.	Abandonment Experiences/Feelings:	sadness; fear; futility.

Like Joyce, Tim never worked through the pain of major loss events in his youth, such as his brother's death and his own Vietnam service. Consequently, as an adult, Tim carried pain from the past, compounded by severe loss conditions in his own family, especially his son's serious illness. At the age of thirty-six, Tim struggled to present himself to the world as a man who loved his family and enjoyed his work as a media technician at a local television station. But, because Tim never learned the emotional skills to heal his feelings, his loss graph clearly depicts a heavy burden of past and present pain.

Joyce and Tim may each continue to carry their increasingly heavy burdens of pain until, one day, they simply can't go on any longer. Or, instead, they may become aware that there is another way of being and another way of dealing with their feelings. With that awareness, that world-view shift, they will be able to turn to a new course for their lives.

Setting Boundaries To Regain Your Power

Once your loss graphs are complete, you have a very graphic representation of your pain and, because you haven't learned the skills to heal your pain, you are also looking at a depiction of your power-lessness. Faced with this picture of your plight, but at the same time, aware now that you can choose a different way of being, where do you begin? One of the first steps is to develop boundaries. Boundaries will give you back your power. Boundaries are the mechanisms that bring safety into our lives by establishing healthy control. Boundaries are statements about what we will and will not do.

Boundaries act as limits for what others can and cannot do to us. By setting boundaries for ourselves, we are exercising our inherent power to declare that we are autonomous individuals in our own right, not possessions or extensions of anyone else.

As a child, you had little power to determine your interactions with the world. You had no way to defend against boundary invasions. Yet, being invaded—used, abused, or violated—you believed you had no personal worth, having been treated as an object or possession, not a person. You may also have believed you were bad or weak because you couldn't stand up for yourself. Believing you are worthless and bad causes tremendous pain. But, now that you are an adult, you can develop and strengthen boundaries, which will give you inner power, and will help heal the old pain.

To let go of the pain, we will have to walk through it to finish it, but we do not have to walk through the pain alone again, as helpless, vulnerable children. But, remember, whatever you experienced as a child, your perceptions and interpretations were those of a child. The perceived belief that you were worthless or bad was not true. You never were bad or unworthy, and you are not today. It is my hope that, in time, you will be able to say and to believe in your heart, "I am good. I am adequate. I am worthy."

WE CAN'T GO FORWARD WITHOUT FINISHING THE PAST

To go forward, we must finish and let go of the past. Jill Johnston, author of *Mother Bound*, writes that as we let go of the past, "we alter the way we see ourselves in the present and the way we cast ourselves into the future....The notion of who has rights, whose voice can be heard, whose individuality is worthy, comes under revision...and the shame of difference will evaporate."

To let go of our pain, we must also acknowledge what we have been doing in the present to control our pain. Facing our own painful reality, both past and present, empowers us by giving us choice.

One option is that we can remain role-players, acting out old family roles, directed by negative judgments and false beliefs about ourselves. Choosing this option, of course, we are not really attempting to finish the past. Also, we are consigning ourselves to a future weighted down by the need to manage our shame and pain.

The other option we have is to become free agents, choosing to set our own course, act according to our own freely chosen beliefs, rather than the dictates of external standards. On this course, we are able to finish the past because we are no longer being controlled by it.

Finishing the past does not mean that it disappears from our memories. Instead, it simply takes its rightful place as one significant dimension of our personal history. And as we release ourselves from the punishing restrictions from our past, our pain is relieved as well. Very simply, if the cause of pain is removed, the pain will subside and then come to an end.

Letting go of our pain doesn't mean that we will, or should be able to forget our suffering. That would be another kind of denial. But, in time we can learn to honor our past pain much as we would honor a soldier returning from war. We can also honor our experience as a significant part of our life's struggle to grow and survive.

Freeing ourselves from pain is what recovery is all about. Releasing ourselves from the past and freeing ourselves from the painful limitations of a past-driven, present life is the process we go through as we turn to the new reality we want. Remember that recovery takes time. But it can be done. It can happen to you, to me, to all of us.

The awarenesses we now have bring us to another turning point to recovery:

The pain we feel is not only from the past, but also from the past-driven present.

We were powerless in the past, but we are not powerless in the present.

Another turning point comes with another awareness:

We are not our pain.

We are much, much more than mere embodiments of pain. Realizing this truth allows us to separate our selves from our emotional responses. Further, our own response is something we can affect, something we can make a choice about. As Steven Covey writes, "Responsibility is response-ability."

Together, these awarenesses lead us to the turning point that can put us on the path of freedom:

Our pain is our responsibility. What we do about our pain is a choice we make.

The remainder of this book will help, guide, and support you through the choice-making process. The next chapter will set the stage for understanding the foundation of the recovery process as the "four steps to freedom." The following chapters will teach the skills to support and care for yourself, as well as new ways of living and being with others, as you learn to give up the old pain-perpetuating beliefs and behaviors and change course to exercising your newly found freedoms.

3
Four Steps to Freedom

The Process of Recovery from Chronic Loss

"It is true that as long as we live we may keep repeating the patterns established in childhood. It is true that the present is powerfully shaped by the past. But it is also true that...insight at any age keeps us from singing the same sad songs again."

—Judith Viorst, *Necessary Losses*

"It is not possible to be honest in the here and now when you continue to discount and minimize your childhood experiences."

—Claudia Black

For adults from troubled families who turn to a new course for their lives, the process of recovery brings renewed energy, new understandings, and new hope.

- Recovery is actively taking responsibility for how you live your life today.
- Recovery is being able to put the past behind. It's no longer having your childhood script dominate how you live your life today.
- Recovery is being able to speak the truth about your growing up years.
- Recovery is the process in which you develop skills you weren't able to learn in your childhood.
- Recovery is a process, not an event, often beginning as a result of a professionally directed treatment or therapy, or experiences in self-help groups.
- Recovery is no longer living a life based in fear or shame.
- Recovery is developing your sense of self separate from survival/coping mechanisms. Your identity is no longer based in reaction, but action.

- Recovery is the process of identifying, owning, and developing healthy ways of expressing feelings; it is the process of learning self-love, self-acceptance. From learning these new ways, a person often learns how to set healthy boundaries and limits, to get needs met, to play, relax, and develop flexibility.
- Recovery is the process of learning to trust yourself and then trusting others, and with trust comes the opportunity for intimacy.

A person is truly on a recovery course when new belief systems and new behaviors are actualized in relationships at work, with friends and family, in the most intimate love and sexual relationships, and in taking care of oneself physically and emotionally. People reach their turning points in different ways. Some begin in Twelve Step programs, others through their religious beliefs, through spiritual healing, and/or professional therapy services. Whatever brings you to your new beginning, you will need to attend to or take care of some major, core issues from your past, so that these are no longer able to dictate how you live your life today.

In chapter 2, we looked at the general causes and the dynamics of past pain, chronic loss, abandonment, fear, and shame. You will need to identify the specific events and conditions in your own life, those that were played out in your past, and those that continue to cause pain in the present. To resolve your feelings and revise your beliefs and re-learn behaviors, you will need to incorporate four identified, important steps that are the backbone of the recovery process. Each time you face a particular issue, you will need to go through all four of these steps.

Four Steps To Recovery

Step One: Explore past losses.
"What happened that hurt me?"
"What didn't I have that I needed?
Step Two: Connect the past to present life.
"How does this past loss influence who I am today?"

Step Three: Challenge internalized beliefs.
"What are the beliefs I internalized from my growing up years?"
"Do I still want to believe that today?"
"Are those beliefs helpful or hurtful to me today?"
"What beliefs do I want to have today?"

Step Four: Learn new skills.
"What do I want to do differently today?"

For some people, simply no longer being part of a hurtful family system, surrounding yourself in healthier emotional environments, creates a spontaneous healing atmosphere in which you begin to feel better about yourself. But the following steps, as key parts of the recovery process, are for the people who find themselves saying, "I really do want to actively work on living my life differently." These people are aware: "There is another reality than the one I live." And they are committed: "I am willing to take some risks so that I can have more freedom in my life."

The steps to recovery, along with the feelings processes and skills needed, are illustrated on the following chart, "Changing Course: The Recovery Process." Each of the four steps will be explained more fully throughout this chapter.

STEP ONE: EXPLORE PAST LOSSES.

"What Happened That Hurt Me?"
"What Didn't I Have That I Needed?

Much of the initial part of the recovery process involves talking about the past. Many people find this both exciting and scary, but some wonder why it is necessary. As I mentioned earlier, if recalling something from the past feels like you have to "drag it up," there is almost always unresolved pain attached to the experience that still affects you today. Clearly, the purpose of talking about the past is to put it behind us.

To let go of the past, you must be willing to break through your denial so you can grieve your pain. In other words, you have to admit to yourself the truth of what happened, rather than hide or keep secret the sadnesses and wounds that occurred. Admitting the truth is not meant to be a process of blaming our parents. In fact, as we go back and explore the past, we may not even choose to share the information with our parents. Whether or not you do is a very individual matter.

Going back to the past is not to assign blame, but to discover and acknowledge reality. Very often, adults still operate on beliefs formed in childhood. Looking back at specific past events, we may come to a major shift in perspective. For instance, if our parents hit us in anger, our childhood assumption was that they were angry at us for something we did wrong or that we were inadequate in some way. As adults, we can see that our parents were really angry with themselves, or angry about something else that had happened, a job loss, for example. As vulnerable children, we were easy targets, so we were the ones who were hit, but for entirely different reasons than we believed.

Our new understanding is critical to re-newing our beliefs about ourselves. However, acknowledging the reality, in this case that our parents hit us, is also essential. One reason is that we will no longer be held hostage by this shameful secret. Another reason is that by acknowledging the reality of what happened, we can feel and grieve the pain.

Exploring the past is very important because it may be the first time in our lives that we have been able to talk openly about our experiences. Often, as we complete our loss graphs we will be able to identify those specific events and conditions that caused pain and restricted our lives. Talking without fear of being rejected or punished allows us to release deep feelings that we have kept inside and that remain hurtful to us. When we do this with other people who are participating in the same process, we receive validation for who we were when we were young. To validate is to give worth to, to declare real and reasonable. The word *validate* comes from the Latin *valere*,

"to make strong." Being validated makes us strong.

Most of us who grew up with chronic loss need to talk with others about our experiences to help us recognize our needs and to learn how to set appropriate limits and boundaries. More important, we are able to discard the messages that we aren't good enough or that we are inadequate. Then, we begin to feel that we are of real value.

A major purpose in going back and talking about the past is to break the denial process, or stop denying the reality you experienced and start speaking the truth. Then you can begin to be honest about what is occurring in the present, in the here and now. It's difficult when you've had to deny, minimize, or discount the first fifteen or twenty years of your life. While denial became a skill that served you as a child in a survival mode, its continued use today interferes in adult experiences.

As an adult, it is easy to continue to minimize, discount, rationalize, but these are behaviors that block the honest identification and expression of feelings, and impede your ability to be honest with yourself and others. This greatly impacts self- esteem and interpersonal relationships. Owning your experiences in childhood greatly relieves the burden of defending yourself as an adult and gives you a beginning of "choice." Exploring the past is an act of empowerment.

GRIEF WORK

The Process For Healing Feelings From The Past

As we discover and acknowledge painful realities in our past, we are, at the same time, doing our "grief work." We are identifying and grieving the losses in our lives. Because the pain of these losses has not been acknowledged or validated, taking the time to grieve for ourselves is important. Left unexamined without appropriate avenues for expression, these feelings of loss grow into emotional time bombs that can become extremely hurtful. We act them out in depression, addictions, compulsive behaviors, hurtful relationships, difficulties with parenting, and so on. It is common to hear people say, "I feel as if something is missing." That something missing is often what we needed, but didn't get.

The classic grief model originated with the work of Dr. Elisabeth Kübler-Ross and since has been expanded by others to encompass a series of universal emotional reactions. The model always begins with LOSS.

From that loss comes SHOCK. We are numb to what has occurred; we disbelieve. We are in DENIAL. We minimize, rationalize; our loss is too painful to acknowledge. Then ANGER results, leading to BARGAINING. This bargaining is often between ourselves and our God or Higher Power.

We feel too helpless to respond. Then DEPRESSION may ensue. GUILT is experienced. Ultimately, we come to ACCEPTANCE.

While adults from troubled families are not grieving death *per se,* but grieving chronic loss, they have their own overlay to this sequence of responses to the classic model of grieving. When LOSS is chronic and there is a likelihood of abandonment at emotionally painful times, we would be more apt to bypass the sense of SHOCK and move into the DENIAL stage more quickly. Often we become so skilled at this we have difficulty even identifying a situation to be a loss. "No, it wasn't important to me that my father didn't come home at night. He would have been drunk anyway." "No, it didn't bother me that my mom slapped me. I was used to it."

ANGER is a natural and healthy response to loss. It is a protest which is an attempt to retrieve that which is gone. But, unfortunately, when people are frightened of rejection, distrusting of their own perceptions, and greatly dependent on others' approval, they have difficulty owning their anger. They don't want to be angry. They want to be understanding. As a result, many people find it easier to move to guilt or depression. Unfortunately, the inability to identify anger interferes with the ability to move through the grief process.

The natural DEPRESSION that is a part of the grief process, whether the grief is from natural loss or chronic loss, is where many people are apt to become stuck. When we face losses with an internal belief that we aren't worthy, we are more apt to succumb to the power of depression and experience a more chronic state of depression.

As you move out of depression it is normal to feel GUILT in response to a loss, and whether or not you are from a troubled family, it is often a false guilt, attempting to take responsibility for that over which we have no control. But, because we have greater difficulty delineating true from false guilt, we are more apt to stay stuck. As a result, we continue to wonder what we could have done to have made things different. "If I had only gone to sleep like I was supposed to..." or "If I had been a good enough kid...." The false guilt we carry with us also keeps us stuck in the BARGAINING stage.

As painful as it is for anyone to wend their way through a grief process, many people find a type of psychological safety in their bargaining. To let go of the bargaining and to reach a healthy place of ACCEPTANCE you have to allow yourself to acknowledge and tolerate of the intensity of your feelings. Acceptance comes as a result of being able to experience each step of this grief process. When it isn't safe to feel, we cannot get to that acceptance.

Now, understanding the grief process and where there is potential to become stuck in the process, you are armed to meet your past or present-day losses. It is necessary to:

1. Identify the losses (the wrongs, the hurts) that happened to us as children. Not only do we grieve the wrongs and hurts, but we often mourn the loss of what we didn't have.

2. Feel our feelings about the losses. That is, we need to experience the felt sense, in addition to identifying and understanding what happened.

3. Embrace and endure those feelings. We need to let them become as big as they really were back then. That is, we must feel the pain all the way through to the deepest levels so no more pain will be left.

4. Share those feelings with others. Sharing our feelings is a way of bringing light and air to the wound to heal it. Shame subsides when a wound is no longer secret; it disappears in the light of another's acceptance.

The process of attending to your losses and grieving your feelings will take weeks, often months, and for some people, maybe years. For most people, it is a process they periodically come back to as specific issues come up at various times.

A COGNITIVE LIFE RAFT AND EMOTIONAL SAFETY NET

Before people are ready to feel the feelings associated with the past, they need to have an intellectual understanding of how past events have affected them. They need to have information about what is "normal," meaning how their environments differed from "normal" environments that did not result in a restricted life of lasting pain. They need to hear others talk about experiences similar to their own. Reading about others' similar experiences also helps so they will have a language to understand and talk about their experiences.

Gaining these insights and understandings allows you to know you are not crazy. You are not bad. There are reasons for your feelings. This process provides a sense of safety and, as described by Dwinell and Moz in their book *After the Tears,* is known as the Cognitive Life Raft. This information will normalize the struggle.

Then you need an Emotional Safety Net. This is when you form a trusting relationship with the person(s) who will guide you through your processs. In order to walk back through the pain, there must be a feeling of trust of self and the trust of at least one significant other with whom to work through the process. While you need to own your fears, sadness, hurt, and anger, you don't necessarily want to do that with your parents; however, you will want to do it with a counselor, other recovering adults, or a trusted friend.

We need to feel safe in order to trust and to share our vulnerabilities. That can take time. For some, it is not so much experiencing our grief that is so lengthy or difficult as it is the process of developing an Emotional Safety Net. In the past, when we trusted someone vital to our emotional well-being, we were betrayed. Consequently, our fear of trusting usually means that we will need time to struggle with our feelings when we begin to trust significant others again. It is this process, however, that eventually leads us to the acceptance and validation of the children we once were.

Compared to the other three steps in recovery process, the first step, which involves exploring and grieving the past, is the most emotionally painful part of recovery. At times, recovering adults have been criticized for focusing on the past too much or for "staying in the problem," as opposed to searching for a solution. However, at this point we are in the process of owning our childhood experiences (grieving losses) and we must take whatever time we need. Everything can't be remembered at the same time, nor do feelings come to the surface all at once.

FEAR OF FEELINGS

Fear of feelings makes it difficult for most of us to talk about the past. Where there is loss, there will be tears. Where there is loss, there will be anger. We must be willing to show our feelings. Feelings don't go away. Repressed feelings only serve to distract us from our real self. We must speak to the sadnesses, the angers, the fears that we never had an opportunity to own or express, and grieve for how we had to live our lives.

You probably have a lot of fear about what will happen if you show your feelings, most likely as a result of what happened when you were a child. If you showed your dad that you were angry, you were apt to get hit across the face or told that you didn't have anything to be angry about. If you showed you were sad, nobody was there to comfort you, to validate that sadness. Maybe you were told to shut up or you were really going to get something to cry about. The people you loved didn't acknowledge when you were embarrassed; in fact, they may have done things to embarrass you, even to humiliate and shame you. No, it was not safe to show your feelings when you were growing up and, as a result, not only do you avoid expressing your feelings now, but often you don't really know what they are.

I've seen people sit with tears streaming down their faces, fists clenched pounding on the desk, and when asked, "What do you feel?"

they respond, "I don't know." While some therapists have understood this to be a kind of resistance, we now realize that some people really do not know. They have been removed from their feelings for so long that they can't identify a feeling.

To help you explore your feelings, here are some questions to ask yourself:

What feelings are easiest for you to show people?

What feeling(s) is difficult for you to show another person?

What do you fear would happen if you showed that difficult feeling?

So often the fear of what would happen if we showed our feeling is the echo of what we feared would happen when we were children.

Sadness

If we get sad, we fear that there will be no one there to comfort us; people will walk away from us or take advantage of us. They will see us as weak or vulnerable, and that is equated to being bad.

As I said earlier, where there is loss there will be sadness, and where there is sadness there will be tears. Tears can be very frightening if you have not cried for five, ten, twenty, or thirty years. Many of us have not cried in a long time. When that is true sometimes we are afraid that if we start crying, we will never stop.

I want you to know that your fears about what will happen when you begin to cry are typically *far greater than the reality*. I have often repeated throughout my years of working with clients that nobody yet has had to be carted out of my office because he or she has cried too hard. You may cry for what seems like eternity, but it will be minutes. The heavy tears are usually three or four minutes, maybe nine or ten minutes. This may make you feel awkward, embarrassed, or afraid, because crying may be a strange experience for you, but nothing bad has to happen. You won't die. You won't go crazy.

When people feel emotionally vulnerable and don't want to be with their feelings, their breathing often becomes very shallow. Soon they are breathing from the chest up, or it seems, from the neck up, rather than from the gut. Then they get a pain in the back of the ears and feel like they are breathing from the ears out.

If this happens to you, it's very important to take slow, deep breaths. Check your breathing. Breathe deeply. When you cry, you may get flushed in the face. Tears may run down and drip off your nose. That's what happens when people cry. But, when you cry, you are going to find that you feel a sense of relief. You won't have as strong a need to be in control and that will feel good. When you cry and when the crying is over, you will find you are not carrying so much of the burden of the world on your shoulders any longer.

Anger

In addition to being afraid of sadness and tears, people often fear their anger. Typically, adults with unresolved pain also have a lot of unresolved anger. Some are very much aware of it. Others are so removed from their anger, they are mystified by the thought. People's fears of what would happen should they express anger are, as with sadness, usually *far greater than the reality,* much greater than what will occur.

When people become angry, their voices may raise, their faces may get flushed, and their bodies tighten. Fear and sadness may accompany the anger. Angry people who don't express their anger often find it eventually gets expressed directly, as in unpredicted outbursts, or indirectly in twisted and distorted ways, such as in overeating, not sleeping, sarcasm, illness or violence.

Adults who have kept their anger stored away are often afraid they'll become angry people. It's not a matter of becoming. It's a matter of owning. The fear I've heard expressed the most is that these people are afraid they are "going to blow somebody away" with their anger. Most adults don't mean that in the literal sense, though they haven't discovered that. When I've asked clients to tell me what that looks like when they "blow someone away," I discover that it most often equates to raising their voices at somebody. Yet, they have this perception that they have the power to blow someone away.

This perception comes from their childhood. When parents got angry, many children felt as if they were going to be blown away. They felt backed up against a wall and helpless. They may have felt as if their whole life was crumbling because of someone else's response. When someone raised a voice or acted irrationally, the child wanted to disappear. When parents yelled, they didn't talk about behavior, they talked about you, your person, your being. They attacked your whole essence. Of course you felt "blown away," especially if this took place when you were developing your sense of worth and identity.

Today, IF you disagree with someone, IF you need to say no to someone, and IF you raise your voice in anger, you have that same sense that you are hurting them in that same fashion as you were hurt as a child. That needs to be put back into perspective. At times, you will raise your voice. You will need to say no. You will need to disagree. You can learn to express anger regarding another's behavior without ever attacking another person's identity, value, or essence. You do not have to do to another what was once done to you.

If there is accumulated anger, it is likely that the initial anger needing to be expressed shouldn't be directed toward the source. It is often helpful to express that anger elsewhere first and then decide whether or not it needs to be directed toward the source. Remember, as you discover your feelings, it is not necessary for you to be alone to figure out how and when to express them. When others are part of your recovery process, they can often offer direction. Here are some questions to help you discover your feelings of anger and sadness:

What picture comes to mind for you when you visualize yourself showing sadness? Showing anger?

What old messages were you given about those feelings?

Are those messages hurting you today? How?

What new messages can you now create for yourself?

If you were raised in a home where people physically hurt other people, or if in your own adult history you have been physically abusive to yourself or others, the fears concerning your anger are naturally greater and have more basis in reality. To make the process of expressing your anger safer and more meaningful for you, the assistance of a professional counselor who can facilitate your anger work is strongly recommended.

Guilt

It is possible that the fear of exploring the past is not about what will happen if you get in touch with sadness or fear, but that you will be certain at last that you are guilty. You still believe there must have been some way you should have been able to influence what happened.

But, as a child growing up in a troubled family, you could not have known then what you know now. Nor could you have changed it. You must stop trying to take on the responsibility of your growing-up years. You were a child and your experiences were influenced and shaped by others. That is the consequence of childhood.

Some of us find it so hard to believe we really couldn't control what happened in our families! Yet, we could not control our childhood. We can influence how it impacts who we are today.

Feeling guilty for other people's behaviors and actions is a "false" guilt. Taking on guilt for things over which we had no control is false guilt. There are enough things in life for which we are responsible and therefore can experience "true" guilt. But believing we were responsible for parental behavior, addictions, compulsions, or believing we should have had the insight or skills of an adult when we were a child or teenager is not one of them.

OVERCOMING THE FEAR OF FEELINGS

Remember, recovery takes time. You don't have to do it all today. When you begin to tell people of your awkwardness or your fears, they won't seem so overwhelming. Feelings are only hurtful when they are denied, minimized, and when they accumulate.

Know that in the beginning as you feel, your feelings come from many sources and some may seem very contrary to each other. You may feel sad and happy at the same time, or sad and angry or loving and hateful. It is possible for all of us to have many contradictory feelings at the same time. You have not gone crazy. It only means you're sad and happy, sad and angry, or that you love and you hate.

Also, trust that there are reasons for the depth of your feelings. Whatever you feel doesn't mean you're bad. What's important is that you are able to talk about those feelings and that you begin to put them out in front of somebody else. You don't have to know the sources of your feelings. But you can open your mouth and say, "I'm sad. I don't know what's going on, but I feel sad." The more you verbalize what you do know and what you feel, the sooner you'll be able to connect your feelings to the sources.

The goal in this process is to be able to discover and acknowledge the reality of what has been lost, to feel the feelings associated with the loss(es), to do this with support, and then to be willing to relinquish the emotional maneuvers that you have used to deny this reality. You need to be able to admit that the loss is permanent. You will never experience the ideal which you so desperately wished for in childhood. While you can do much today to get many of those needs met, no amount of experience or grieving will completely erase how it was "then." Ultimately, this allows you to be willing to withdraw your emotional investment in that which has been lost and move on in your recovery process.

It is usually early in the discovery process that the pain may seem overwhelming, but it will pass as you are willing to identify it and own it. It is very important that you have a support system, people you can talk to regularly about these feelings. Talking, rather than keeping the feelings within, often takes the power out of the feelings. Receiving validation from others lessens the pain as well.

As you begin to experience these pent-up feelings from the past, go ahead and fully feel those feelings. As intense as the pain can be, trying to control and defend those feelings prolongs the pain. Allow yourself the feelings. Own them and be with them. Remember that a lot of what you are experiencing is the accumulation of many years of feelings—feelings that previously were not safe to experience. This does take time, but people who actively pursue self-discovery in a therapy or self-help environment find that usually within six to eight months, the pain has greatly lessened.

In those times of great feeling, you may need to take deliberate steps to lessen external stresses. This is no time to take on added responsibilities. Make more time for yourself. Stay aware that this is a vulnerable time—it is a passage that does not last forever. Now is the time to treat yourself with kindness.

Exploring your past and grieving the pain associated with your losses are vital to recovery, but it is just as important that eventually you move beyond this first step. If not, you will become stuck in the process and it will then become a blaming process, not a grief process.

Talking about your childhood is not the complete answer to changing the course of your life. This is a time of much insight, awareness, and understanding of ourselves and others. It is a time of hope and realizing we have greater choices available. Hopefully, the talking and new awarenesses will bring us to our turning point. But once we reach that point, we must take steps in the new direction.

From exploring the past and grieving the past pain, three other steps are vital for our recovery.

STEP TWO: CONNECT THE PAST TO PRESENT LIFE.

"How Does This Past Loss Influence Who I Am Today?"

Connecting your past to the present is more of a rational, insight-oriented process than an emotional process. The cause-and-effect connections you discover between your past losses and present life will give you a sense of direction. It allows you to become more centered in the here and the now. This clarity will identify the areas you need to work on — where pain still affects you, where you are missing the skills needed to get free of the influences and restrictions from the past.

As you work on answering the question, "How does my past affect who I am today?" you become increasingly centered in the here and now. Also, you will need to address that question to various areas of your life, such as:

How does my past affect who I am as a parent?

How does that affect who I am in the work place?

How does that affect who I am in a relationship?

How does that affect how I feel about myself?

These are questions we seldom take time to ask ourselves, but the answers are vital in our recovery. It is helpful to take the time to write your responses. Growing up with shame, you have had a tendency to intellectualize most things. By writing, you may find yourself more vulnerable and, as a result, more honest. And as you work on this step in your recovery, you need to make each question even more detailed. Here are some suggested, more specific questions for the general areas of self, relationships, parenting, and the work place:

1. How does the fact that I lived with chronic loneliness for the first twenty years of my life affect how I feel about myself today? How does that affect me in the context of my relationships? ...friendships? ...in my parenting skills?

2. How does the fact that I was so fearful of making mistakes in my childhood affect me today in my work? in my play? as a parent?

3. How does the fact that, as a child, I was always looking for approval from somebody affect me today in my parenting? in

my relationships? at work?

4. How does the fact that I spent so much time in isolation and a fantasy world as a child affect me today? in my expectations of myself? my choice of friends?

5. How does the fact that the only way I could find safety was to create a fantasy world affect me in my choice of careers?

6. How does the fact that I lived with chronic fear affect me today in these areas of my life?

7. How does the fact that it was never safe to express my anger affect me in these areas?

8. How does the fact that I lived with a mother who was emotionally cold, a father who was never satisfied with what I did, affect me today?

These are the kinds of questions we need to ask ourselves and the kinds of questions that create a cause-and-effect connection between our childhood years and our lives today.

We often make assumptions about one of the areas of our lives without going through the exploration process. For example, we may assume that since "work is good," and "I am doing a good job," we don't need to explore that area. But, by asking ourselves these questions in Step Two, linking the past to how we function in the present, often we discover ways that we continue to perpetuate pain or repeat old behaviors that hinder rather than help us. By asking, "How does the fact that I used school and keeping busy to detract from my loneliness relate to my work today?" we may find that we are presently using work as the detractor that school once was. We may work sixteen hours every day for weeks, and then reward ourselves by going on a food or alcohol binge, or a spending binge, seemingly to reward ourselves for a job well done. Very likely we did do a good job at work, but what we have done even better is add to our load of shame—another ten pounds gained, another drunk-driving ticket, another outrageous credit card debt, and a closet full of clothes we don't need and, or really want.

While this step connecting the past and present offers us insight, it also will bring up feelings. For instance, think about what it means to be forty-five years old today, and still afraid to make a decision. How does that make you feel about your adequacy? Further, what if you haven't learned to listen? How has that interfered in relationships with intimate partners? And, what do you feel when you try to identify your needs? The answers to such questions bring up a lot of pain.

Sherry, a client, reflected,"It was so hard to be with my pain, because I realized the fantasy life I created for myself as a child has been what has kept me so unrealistic in terms of my life goals. I realized it never felt safe to make a decision and that is still true today!" We are often grateful to understand the past-present connection and find it useful to be able to recognize how old messages and experiences still dictate our lives. Yet, we also need to own the anger we may have about that, or the sadness that accompanies the insight, or even the fear that comes with now wanting to change certain patterns. We need to connect the past to the present. And, as we do that, we need to feel the feelings, identify the source of the feelings, and grieve the pain.

STEP THREE: CHALLENGE INTERNALIZED BELIEFS.

"What Are The Beliefs I Internalized From My Growing Up Years?"
"Are Those Beliefs Helpful Or Hurtful To Me Today?"
"What Beliefs Do I Want To Have Today?"

Beliefs we internalized in our growing up years often continue to determine our behaviors without our being aware. These messages were often parental attitudes and value statements that became "shoulds." First, we need to identify the beliefs and then we need to ask ourselves whether these messages are positive or negative, helpful or hurtful, to how we want to live our life today. We need to question whether or not these internalized messages are messages that we want to continue to take with us throughout our adulthood.

So, we begin this step asking, "What do I believe about
_____?" and then we must challenge our answers: "Is that a
belief that is helpful to me today?" or "Is that a belief that is harmful
to me now?"

Examples of beliefs that we often learned at a young age that are
hurtful to us are:

I can't trust anybody.

Nobody is ever going to be there for me.

I am not important.

I am not of value. I better do things right because if I don't, something bad is going to happen.

My needs are not important. Everyone else's are far more important.

There's no time to play. I have to get things done.

I am *supposed* to take care of others.

I can't do anything, so don't bother.

Whatever I do, it's never good enough.

You may find it helpful to check these kinds of beliefs. It's also a
good time to challenge any other beliefs that were formed from your
experience, and may be hurtful now.

These hurtful, internalized messages interfere with skill-build-
ing. For example, if you truly believe your needs aren't important, it
will be difficult to learn to express your needs. If you believe you
can't do anything and/or it's never good enough, you won't initiate,
that is, try anything new on your own. If you believe your job is to
take care of others, you will very likely neglect yourself. It's going
to be important to identify a certain message and to decide—to
choose—whether or not this is a message you want to keep.

Once hurtful messages are identified, you need to let them go
symbolically. Many adults changing course skip over this part of the
step. They explore the past, they connect the past to the present, they
try to learn some skills, but they don't actively look at the messages

they have internalized. And sometimes when they do look at a message, and identify it, they don't actively get rid of it.

There are many ways to symbolically get rid of on old belief. Write the message down and tear it up. Write it down on a piece of poster paper, put it in a chair, and say No to it. Do a visualization of the belief; i.e., visualize the belief and watch it disintegrate. If you play computer games, put the piece of paper with the message on it into a playing field and bomb it. Another way to get rid of a belief symbolically is to do some type of ritual exercise to let go of it. Develop a ritual that works for you. It is important for you to get actively involved in letting the message go. The purpose is serious, but the process here can be fun.

After the ritual of letting go of the old belief, replace the belief with a healthy message. Here are some examples of old, unchallenged beliefs replaced with beliefs you choose.

Old, Inaccurate Belief	*New, Revised Belief*
"People aren't trustworthy."	"Most people can be trusted."
"I have to say Yes or people will think I am weak."	"I can say No and still be a strong person."
"There is no time to play."	"Time to play is important."
"Mistakes mean I'm a failure."	"Mistakes mean I'm only human."

Although you need to replace negative beliefs, you probably received some helpful messages from your family. It will be just as important to ascertain what those were. You may have heard from your father that you were special, of value. Or, that you could do whatever it is that you wanted to do (high expectations). You may have heard the Golden Rule: "Do unto others as you want them to do unto you." Many times these are messages that you would like to continue to take with you in life. When that is true, you need to take ownership of the beliefs.

You need to know what *you* believe, not just your father's (or mother's) belief system that you have internalized. You need to literally say, "That's what my father told me and that's been very helpful to me and now I believe that for myself." You don't need to hear them just as your father's message for you. You will take ownership of the message, the value. "I am capable, I am special, I'm of value and I can do whatever I set my mind to doing." The baton has been turned over to you, so to speak, and you are now responsible for carrying this message.

Once you have discovered any "parental beliefs" or "shoulds" you have internalized that are getting in the way of how you want to live your life, toss them out. But again, know that while this begins as more of an intellectual search, you will have feelings that need to be felt. Identifying that you have lived with the message "My needs aren't important" is something to be angry about. Recognizing that you have experienced "No one wants to listen to what I have to say" is very sad. As you reframe a healthier message in the place of the old message, you must work through the emotions of change.

Be cautious as you work on this step, because it is the one people are most likely to skip over and neglect. It can appear insignificant or trivial. In general, a strong emotional reaction is not created, so there is not the level of excitement some people expect in recovery. Depending on which issue you are addressing, it can be very "emotionally loaded," but that is not the main idea of this step. The point is that it is vital to address your issues and take more responsibility for how you live your life today.

It is through working on these three steps that you are ready to truly learn and incorporate new behaviors or skills into your life.

STEP FOUR: LEARN NEW SKILLS

"What Do I Want To Do Differently Today?"

The fourth step is about learning skills. [Note that the skills referred to here are the wide variety of skills generally needed to meet various situations. In chapter 4 we will discuss the fine skills specifically needed to go forward and grow stronger as we work through these four recovery steps.] Ultimately, our life changes when we learn and practice skills or behaviors—things we can learn to do to take care of ourselves and to have healthy relationships with others—that we didn't learn in our earlier years. "I want to be a better listener," "I want to learn to solve problems better," "I want to be able to see options," "I want to learn to negotiate better." These are living skills and "people skills," ways of being with your self and with others.

People will often want to bypass the first three steps and simply get on with learning new skills. Most of us are in a hurry to move on in our lives, and that is understandable. Ever since childhood, we have been anxious to leave the present moment in anticipation of the next day, because we were certain it had to be better. We don't want to grieve, or to take time to be insightful about connecting the past to the present, or to spend time doing what appears to be a trivial exercise of challenging our beliefs. This urgency applies to a great many of us. We are in a hurry. We have other things to do.

While to some extent you can rush your process, so to speak, by immersing yourself in behavior change programs, most people find that if they do not do each step in successive order as it is attached to an issue, they won't follow through with learning the new skill because there is an emotional component to each skill that has not been addressed.

Let's say, for example, that you want to do a better job of setting limits for yourself. You want to be more assertive because you are feeling victimized in certain situations. But what happens is this: You can learn assertiveness techniques and skills, but very likely you won't follow through and actually use those skills, because you haven't dealt with the issues of the fear of rejection and the need for approval. Those are the emotional issues connected to the skill.

Or you want to learn how to ask others for help. You can identify safe people, develop a behavioral hierarchy identifying a list of items or issues to ask for help with, but unless you deal with how frightening it was to ask for help as a child, you won't follow through with practicing the new skill.

Your intellect or rational mind will now know what to do to bring about the result you want, but your underlying emotions will impede your actually choosing to act in that new way. The new behavior won't follow until the emotional component underlying the old behavior has been dealt with. That's what happens in the first three steps—you deal with those old beliefs and fears. You then create a new belief system that supports the new behavior, the new skill you want to learn.

As we change course, we go through a process where, ultimately, we withdraw our emotional investment in what has been lost and take responsibility for taking care of and respecting ourselves. That self-care and self-respect is created by developing and reframing beliefs that are supportive of our emotional and physical health, and then by learning the skills that act on these new beliefs, taking personal responsibility for getting our needs met.

Learning Adult Skills As A Child

Children in troubled families did learn skills. In fact, sometimes they learned skills that other children didn't. Some learned to cook at a particularly young age. Others became very skilled at controlling their emotions. Many developed strong listening skills. They also became creative in their problem-solving and very self-reliant.

Often, we were responding to situations as if we had the skills of an adult, but we were still children. Unfortunately, the skills we learned in a troubled home were often skills and behaviors that were premature for our age or from a basis of fear or shame. When that occurs, there is a tendency to feel like an imposter. Also, because we developed skills from a premise of fear or shame, and because we learned due to an immediate need, we were often limited in options and problem-solving. This commonly translates to being very rigid in how we handle situations as adults. So now, while we have skills, we don't have flexibility. We have a sense of urgency about what we're doing: "I had better do this, and I'd better do it right. I can't make a mistake, because if I do, something bad is going to happen." We are skilled, but we feel a sense of urgency, with fear and shame close behind.

It is important to take a look at the skills you did learn, and to be open to developing those even more fully, with the input of other people today and with healthier role models than you had in your childhood and teenage years.

Take a moment to list skills you learned growing up. Then, take a look at the skills that you did not learn. Usually these skills are very basic, but are vital to being able to address more complex skills in adult life.

To help you begin to look at your own experience, here are some of the behaviors or skills children need to learn:

1) asking for help

2) expressing feelings appropriately

3) setting limits

4) saying no

5) validating yourself

6) initiating

7) asking questions

8) negotiating

9) problem-solving

10) taking charge

11) listening

12) playing

Adult skills are often taken for granted, except by those who may not have had the opportunity to develop them. If we did not learn these skills as a child and adolescent, we move into adulthood forced to experience ourselves as if an imposter. We try to hide our performance anxiety, fear of change, and fear of problem-solving, spending a great amount of time and energy manipulating our environment so we don't have to be confronted with what we perceive to be our "insufficiency." But, often we didn't know or didn't understand there was another way to be.

Recovery offers you the opportunity to acknowledge what you need to learn.

To say, "I did not learn this very basic skill and I need to know how" is a turning point.

Then you can begin to practice.

Feelings Associated With Learning Skills

Learning skills is much more behavioral than emotional, yet like the other steps there will be feelings associated. As you now know, you must allow your feelings about the past to emerge full force into the present. But also, you must feel your feelings about the present—those that come with your behavior in the present. You will have feelings in the present as you identify and recover from the current ways you have been trying to control you, pain from the past. Also, you will have other feelings, such as awkwardness and unfamiliarity, as you try your new skills and as you relate to other people in your newly discovered ways.

To be an adult and have to go back to learn basic skills at this point in your life brings up a lot of different, painful emotions. Each and every possible time you have a feeling, you must stop, pay attention to it—honor it. You need to 1) feel the feeling; 2) identify the source of the feeling, and 3) express it in the here and now. You will need to go through this process consciously until doing so becomes habit, until you consistently meet your own needs. Here are some pertinent questions to think about to help bring your feelings to the surface:

—If, as an adult, you are in the process of learning to make decisions, how does it make you feel having to learn that skill now? Afraid? Angry? Sad?

—If you are just now learning to listen to your significant others—family, friends, and intimate partner—how do you feel about the problems that were created by your inability to be open to hearing them?

Sad? Guilty? Regretful?

—When you try now to identify your own needs, how does that make you feel?

Confused? Insecure? Uncertain? Afraid?

—Not knowing your own needs surely means these needs weren't being met and, as a result, your neediness must have affected your relationship. What feelings do you have about now trying to have your needs met in your relationship?

Fear? Confusion? Insecurity?

Each of the feelings you name as you answer these questions includes a lot of pain. When you begin to practice the skills that allow you to take care of yourself, you often feel vulnerable as a child who is just learning to read, and you may be even more embarrassed. You are no longer that child, and so you want to tell yourself you "should" be able to do these things. Remember, this is not about "shoulds." Maybe when you were growing up, it was not safe to have learned a certain skill, such as assertiveness. Or perhaps there were no models of this skill to learn from. Whatever your circumstances, you coped and survived as best as you could, and it was not until later in life that you could recognize that you lacked these kinds of skills.

APPLYING THE FOUR STEPS TO A RECOVERY ISSUE

With each and every issue you address in recovery, you will usually have to take these four steps. Let's use, as an example, that saying No is a problem for you now because of what you experienced when you said No as a child. Here's what your process might look like:

Step One: Explore past losses.
How did you hear No as a child?
Who did you hear it from?
What did that experience mean to you as a reflection of your worth?
Of your parents' care for you?
What happened when you said No as a child? How did that make you feel?

Step Two: Connect the past to the present.
How does your past experience affect you in the different areas of your life today?
When do you have difficulty saying No?
How do you feel when you say No?

Step Three: Challenge internalized beliefs.
What were the messages you got around No?
Take ownership of the helpful beliefs.
Cast out the hurtful messages.
Create new, constructive belief around the word No.

Step Four: Learn new skills.
Identify situations when you would like to say No.
Rank these from easiest to most difficult.
Practice the experience of saying No, beginning with the easiest and building up to the most difficult.

In the example above, the four steps were applied to the problem of saying No. Here is another example of using the four steps, applied to difficulty in initiating:

Step One: Explore past losses.
What happened if you tried to initiate as a child?
What did you fear would happen?

Step Two: Connect the past to the present.

How does not initiating today impact you in different areas of your life?

What could you have in your life today if you did initiate?

Step Three: Challenge internalized beliefs.

As a child, what messages did you get about initiating?

Cast out the hurtful messages.

Create new beliefs that support you taking initiative versus being passive.

Step Four: Learn new skills.

Identify areas you would like to take more initiative in.

Place in a hierarchy from what seems easiest/safest to begin with to most difficult/scariest.

Begin with safest, building up confidence to be able to respond to most difficult.

RECOVERY CAN'T BE RUSHED

We are often in a hurry to move on in our lives, and that is very understandable. Ever since childhood, we have been anxious to leave the present moment in anticipation of the next day, because we were certain it had to be better.

People will often want to bypass the first three steps of the recovery process and simply get on with the fourth step, learning new skills. They don't want to explore the past and to grieve, to take time to learn about connecting the past to the present, and to spend time doing what appears to be a trivial exercise of challenging beliefs.

We are in a hurry, but we need to be willing to prioritize our recovery. That means taking the time to walk through each step of the process.

Be kind to yourself. Give yourself credit. Remember, as you work the recovery process, you are working the four steps to freedom.

TURNING POINT:

Recovery isn't changing who you are.

It is letting go of who you are not.

4
Building Your Own Inner Adult

Skills To Create A Core Of Personal Strength

"Only when you withdraw from others can you return to them in a place that is truly your own."

—Sheldon Kopp,
All God's Children Are Lost, But Only a Few Can Play the Piano

"It is in knowing what your needs are that they are most apt to be met."

—Claudia Black

The late actor Anthony Perkins described himself as terrified of women until he was forty. It took years of therapy, Perkins said, before he overcame his crippling fear, which he blamed directly on his domineering mother. "She wasn't ill-tempered or mean," he explained, "just strong-willed, dominant....She controlled everything about my life, including my thoughts and feelings. 'What are you reading? Now where are you going?' She felt she was taking responsibility, but she was really taking control."

Television actress and entertainer Suzanne Somers wrote of her childhood: "My father was drunk the day I was born. By the time I was born, he was well into 'the hates.' My dad turned a lot of his self-loathing outward. He'd show up at school assemblies and shout obscenities at the nuns. Sometimes during our priest's sermon at Sunday Mass, I'd hear my dad's unmistakable voice at the back of the church. He'd be talking too loud, swearing at the priest. I felt ashamed, as if the outbursts were my fault. It took away my dignity."

These two accounts describe the kinds of family environments where children's personal boundaries and core identities are threatened at very young ages, when they are just beginning to develop a sense of a personal self and self-worth. The questions children must struggle to answer are universal and central to all of us: "Who am I?...Am I an extension of my mother, a possession of my father, or a real and separate individual?" "How much am I worth?...Am I loved? Am I lovable?" "What do I think and feel?...What happens when I tell my parents my secret fears?" "When can I say no?...Or do I always have to say yes in order to be loved...for if I am not loved, surely I will be abandoned, and if I am abandoned, surely I will die."

These central questions create our sense of self, and the answers we settle on are determined largely by the responses from those around us. In situations like those above and in many millions of other families, children are given negative answers, or mixed messages, or no answers at all, which may be the most devastating kind of parental response. Without answers from those we love, the people we depend on for survival, the questions are left to echo in our dark interior self until we attempt, through our own childhood logic, to guess at an answer.

CREATING AN INNER HOLDING ENVIRONMENT

Although the specifics are different in everyone's lives, we do know a great deal about the dynamics that are common within troubled families. We know that something, some event or some force, has disrupted the natural order of their lives. An event might be death of a parent or divorce, with the consequences of a parent's debilitating depression, or drastically reduced living conditions for the family. A force might be as blatantly harmful as drug addiction or subtle and deceptively benign—a strict religious code of behavior, for example.

In the midst of chaos, rigidity, or a combination of the extremes, and in the absence of strong, positive parental messages to the contrary, children conclude that they are not of value and that they may at any time be abandoned. These two things in combination are the source of almost unbearable shame.

We are often desperate in our attempts to hide our core self, because we feel damaged or loathsome. Unbeknownst to us, other children had early daily encounters with loving, good-enough mothers and fathers, so they felt safely held, both physically and emotionally. They were able to build up memories of being cared for and about that became integral parts of themselves, that they internalized, which then formed their core beliefs about and behaviors toward themselves. These core beliefs and behaviors are the ones we will have to learn on our own, because as Judith Viorst writes: "We cannot stand alone until we come to possess this inner holding environment." The core beliefs and behaviors that create this "inner holding environment" are the core recovery skills, built around a core of positive regard for ourselves and the willingness to nurture our inner being.

CORE RECOVERY SKILLS

New awarenesses of what is possible can bring you to the turning point in your life. One of those awarenesses is that an inner core of worthlessness is not all there is for you. Another is that while this may have been your legacy, you are not helpless to change course now. It is very important to remember, though, that you are not changing who you are. You are changing certain beliefs and behaviors— you are changing how you see yourself and how you take care of your pain!

Using the four steps discussed in chapter 3, you will be able to have a basic understanding of how you came to believe you are inadequate, how your past has been affecting your life, and how you can challenge and change old beliefs and behaviors for your present and future. Now you are ready to learn the skills you need to take care of yourself on your course to recovery—a recovery from an impaired lifestyle adopted as a result of impaired original beliefs and inaccurate present beliefs that were the basis of the counterproductive behaviors, past and present.

Core Recovery Skills

(1) Validate yourself
(2) Let go of some control
(3) Feel your feelings
(4) Identify your needs
(5) Set limits and boundaries

These are the skills that everyone needs, but you did not learn because, whether all or in part, these were missing when you were growing up. Because you did not receive validation, you did not feel validated and, with a child's logic, you concluded that you were not worthy of being validated. During the very early stages of your development, and without other messages to the contrary, there was no way for you to conclude anything else. It is beyond the realm of possibility for children to wonder whether the parents themselves are incapable of offering what the children need, for the family is the child's universe—the be all and end all to their experience—until they get old enough and mature enough to conceive of other possibilities.

When chaos prevailed—because of a raging alcoholic or because parents were literally absent in the home for whatever reason—your physical survival was in jeopardy. When rigidity was the order, your emotional survival was at risk, and possibly your physical survival, since severe punishment often followed misbehavior. Whatever the case in your family, whether in chaos, rigidity, or somewhere between these extremes, the first priority was literally to save yourself, so you tried in every way possible to be in control of what happened to you, and also to others at risk—your younger brothers and sisters, for example.

Of course, when your natural feelings were discounted, shamed, or punished, you simply hid them, and then kept hiding them deeper and deeper until you didn't seem to feel them any more. Along with no longer recognizing your own feelings, you also learned to ignore your needs. After all, your parents' needs and wants came first. If your parents or others in your family were sucked into a system of addiction and codependency, children were simply caught up in following the rules of protection and denial, as well as caretaking the parents and themselves. If the central dynamic of the system was some kind of obsession with a religious code, children's needs were probably not acknowledged as legitimate, and any deviance from the code was a sin.

Whatever was true in your family, others set your limits and tried to invade the boundaries of your core self, maybe the boundaries of your physical self. Almost inevitably, these intrusions were confusing and painful.

But, knowing how it was for you and how it might have been—had your parents been different, but they weren't—you can compensate by learning these recovery skills on your own. You are, in essence, becoming your own parent.

In truth, we all parent ourselves when we become adults. We have internalized beliefs and behaviors that either echo our parents or are in opposition to them, as we try to compensate for the negative effects we felt.

Rather than look back in anger at what we did and didn't learn, or look with envy at what others did learn, we can simply begin with the premise that all of us act as either loving or unloving parents to ourselves now.

Parenting ourselves is a concept that feels artificial to some and off-putting to some others—maybe because we have negative memories of being parented, and so that's the last thing we want to go through again! However, let's not get stuck in the connotations of the words *parent* and *child,* and just take a careful look at how we treat ourselves. We either put ourselves down or build ourselves up; we treat ourselves badly or we take care of ourselves. But now, we can consciously decide what we want to do for ourselves or, if you will, what kind of parent we want to be. We can decide what we want to believe, and feel, and do about ourselves—and go from there.

The new awareness that we can *choose* how we want to treat ourselves is simple and clear. The difficulty occurs when we actually put into action such things as revising old beliefs and acting in a new and appropriate manner when an upsetting event or conflict arises. Each experience is one part of the whole renewal process, a process that is gradual and takes time.

"Passion And Gradualness"

Taking steps one at a time is a natural learning process that builds on itself. If we by-pass the individual steps, jumping into situations before we learn how to handle them, we won't be able to reach our goals. For example, we may hope to have intimacy in our relationships, but we may not have learned yet how to express our feelings. Or, we want to be the perfect parent, but we never learned how to set limits for ourselves, let alone our children. However, rather than be hard on ourselves for wanting too much, too soon, we can remind ourselves that all great enterprises—and rebuilding our lives is certainly a great enterprise—require two things, according to Albert Schweitzer, "passion and gradualness."

Being raised in a troubled family often meant being raised in a family where your sense of safety was unsure. You couldn't trust that you were going to be physically protected. Because of that, you didn't feel psychologically safe. You didn't feel the protection that children need to experience in order to be willing to risk assertive behavior. You didn't feel the protection children need to experience to be willing to risk sharing what they feel and need. Safety to share and to risk are elements that nurture a person's growth. It is my hope that as you change course now, you will find recovery to be a safe process. That does not mean your life will be pain-free or necessarily easy, but that you will feel safe to risk and grow.

There are different ways that people approach recovery, just as there are different ways to learn other skills. Take swimming, as an example. If I wanted to teach children to swim, there are different ways to do that. It is possible to take children out on a raft in water ten feet over their heads, throw them over the side, and expect them to swim back to shore. While many children would make it back to shore, it is very possible that some would not be able to and would be in danger of drowning, so this is a very harsh way to teach, a hard way to try to learn.

The recovery process does not need to be so harsh. When you learn the core recovery skills, you build the foundation for your "inner holding environment." Practicing these skills will allow you to face the core causes of your pain without feeling like you will drown in your emotions. It is as if you are learning to swim with a sense of safety, starting in shallow waters and developing your self-confidence as you go deeper.

It is my hope in early recovery that you quickly begin to practice self-validation and self-approval. That paves the way for you to feel safer as you explore more fully the issue of control, confronting your need to stay in control and learning to let go little by little. Letting go of control quickly leads to dealing with the issue of feelings. At the point you begin to identify and express feelings, you will start to identify your needs. Then, to get needs met, you must begin to set limits and boundaries. As you do these things, you are developing a sense of self—a sense of who you really are. Self-worth is increasing. Shame is lessening. A foundation of positive self-regard is being constructed.

This foundation will offer you the safety to go to greater depths within yourself, which, in turn, will take you further on the course of your recovery. As you proceed to build the strength of your inner core, you will undoubtedly still be frightened of letting go of some control. With this and other very difficult issues, I want you to have some comfort with your feelings. If you start to cry, I want you to know that you are not going crazy. And if you are angry, you don't have to self-destruct. I want you also to be able to identify what you need.

Very often people feel the need to jump into all of their issues at once, and that is like experiencing "emotional" or "cognitive" surgery without medical help or preparation. When that occurs, the consequences are so frightening that people often just stop their efforts to work through their pain. They may become so afraid of what they are feeling, they won't risk trying again. By taking steps one at a time, the "gradualness" provides the safety to continue in the process.

Orderly Overlap

These recovery skills can't really be worked on in a compartmentalized fashion. You can not do all the work that is necessary in one area—validating yourself, for example—before to moving on to another skill, such as identifying your needs. Human emotions are not that simple, and human behavior is not constant or absolute. Our issues will easily overlap, and in working through them, we need to use different skills in different combinations. Yet, as beginners, when we set out to learn the skills, the concept of order is still valid.

Recovery Steps And Recovery Skills Overlay Each Other

Recalling the four steps to recovery presented in the previous chapter, picture the recovery skills as an overlay to the recovery steps. In other words, when you work a step, such as connecting the past to the present, you will need to use recovery skills, such as validating yourself.

Also, you will need to work through the four steps so you can come to terms with your having to learn these basic skills now. Here is an example of the four recovery steps applied to a childhood loss—the inability to validate yourself:

Step One: You need to describe how validation was or was not experienced, and whether your feelings were or were not expressed. Then you'll need to grieve the pain associated.
Step Two: Now connect your past inability to validate yourself with the present. How has that affected you today?
Step Three: Next, identify specific beliefs you have internalized about your self-worth. Challenge your beliefs with questions such as, "Is my personal worth determined by things outside of myself—other people? my job? etc."
Step Four: Finally, once you acknowledge that you do, in fact,

have worth as an individual human being, practice the skill of validating yourself; for example, by repeating, "I am a whole human being with a wide range of thoughts and feelings. I accept and love myself—my body, my thoughts, my feelings— just the way that I am, and I know that I am worthy."

Applying the four recovery steps to each of the recovery skills is very helpful to people in all stages of their personal growth. Sometimes people get stuck as they work through a painful issue. If you experience yourself as stuck, or having reached a plateau, you may find it helpful to go back and spend more time applying the steps to the recovery skills. It can be helpful to visualize resolution of your past losses around these skills as setting the foundation to your recovery process.

Resistances To Learning Recovery Skills

Before you venture further, if you feel resistant to recovery, there are probably two primary reasons, and they will become evident at this time. I find the greatest sources of resistance are:

(1) We want recovery, but we'd like the process to be pain-free.
(2) We want recovery, but we would prefer to do it by ourselves.

We would all like to avoid going through emotional pain—I know I certainly would. But we need to own and feel that which has been harbored in our body and soul so we can set it free. And, as we will soon discuss, our *fear* of feelings is often more powerful than anything that actually occurs when we feel. As an Adult Child, know you never again have to walk through the pain as a child and you never again have to walk through the pain alone.

While you would like to reach recovery alone, recognize that you have lived a life of isolation. So, wanting to go through this process alone often reflects the rigid self-reliance you learned, as well as not having learned to trust. You deserve to have help by allowing others to be a part of your process. There are many who will understand your emotional struggles and pain. Whether you choose to begin your recovery with a therapist, a Twelve Step group, or in treatment, there are literally millions of others who understand your resistances because they have struggled, too.

The awarenesses that have brought you to your turning point are much like a sailboat changing course. The boat simply "comes about," turns to a new direction, and the wind refills the sails. As you change course, the steps you now know along with the skills you are learning will harness or guide the power of the wind to help you move along your newly chosen way.

You have the opportunity to turn now.
You deserve to begin rebuilding your life in a new direction.

The recovery skills listed earlier in this chapter are guiding and rebuilding skills. The following explanations will enhance your understanding of each one.

VALIDATING YOUR SELF

As soon as possible, we must begin the process of actively valuing and approving ourselves. If, as children, we did not learn that we had worth, then we need to gain a sense of worth in order to feel we are worth the recovery process.

A part of recovery is to become independent of the need for other people's approval. As a group, people raised in troubled families are often highly dependent upon others' approval and on what others think of them. It is important to become self-validating so that we are not so dependent on others, but also because it allows us to see movement in our process of recovery. It allows us to see that, in fact, we are doing things differently now than we have done them in the past. It allows us to see our progress, and that gives us something for which to celebrate. It also gives us a sense of hope, direction, and helps to keep us in the process.

Yet, most of us are harshly critical of ourselves. Unless we do something as significant as move a mountain, it is never good enough. And then if we do move the mountain, unless there are people there applauding, it is never good enough. Few people in their lifetimes ever move mountains, but if they do, they do it with the help of a lot of other people and by taking a lot of little steps. Yet, it isn't the mountain getting moved that makes the difference. It is the little steps along the way.

Earlier I mentioned the tendency for people to take recovery in leaps and bounds. This is understandable, because so much of our life has been experienced in extremes and with unrealistic expectations. We have often lived our life from a "one and ten" perspective, an all or nothing way of being, feeling, living.

Recovery is learning the numbers two through nine.

We need to accept and validate ourselves for being who we are. Because we can never be perfect, we are not doomed to failure. We must accept both our power and powerlessness in life.

We deserve to experience our personal growth, to celebrate, to feel good about ourselves. Yet, it is so difficult to be self-approving when, as a child, you learned that no matter what you did, it was never good enough. We don't need anyone today to reinforce that what we do is never good enough; we have internalized it. We repeat that message to ourselves. As children, we needed our parents to tell us specifically what was likeable, lovable about us. We needed our parents to applaud us for just being. Parents are often critical of their children, very abrupt in their responses, and often simply don't notice the little things or even the big things that help children feel good about who they are.

One child comes home from school, looking forward to telling her mother about the day, to find Mom passed out on the couch. Another child comes home to tell his mother something that made him feel good that day, and finds Mom on the couch crying. In either case, the children aren't going to be acknowledged, supported, or validated. Their needs are ignored, and they are recognized only when they try to take care of their mother.

Another child brings home his report card which shows he has done extremely well. He is anxious to show it to Dad, seeking Dad's approval, but Dad doesn't come home that night. In fact, three days go by before Dad returns. Do you think anyone remembers then that this thirteen-year-old boy has brought home his report card? Does anyone care? No, everybody is focused on Dad—where he has been, what he was doing, and what will happen now.

When children are developing their sense of worth and their identity, they experience their personal value by others' verbal responses, or failure to respond, and others' behavior toward them. Children need to know what is good about their behavior and themselves. "I need to know that I am special. I am of value. I am important." They consistently need to hear words that affirm this. When that does not occur, children do not internalize a sense of worth, value, or accomplishment.

As an adult, you need to begin validating yourself as a part of your own reparenting process. When people can truly begin to validate themselves simply for being who they are, then they will not have to continue to seek approval outside of themselves.

When you first begin to look back at your early loss conditions, such as the absence of validation, it is easy to get overwhelmed by personal pain. Consequently, people often comment they wish they were still in denial. People talk about entering the tunnel of recovery and rather than seeing light at the end, they feel the tunnel closing in around them, getting darker. If this happens to you, it may help to remember this:

By recognizing that you are in the process of recovery, you are beginning to shine your own light.

You deserve to have a sense of moving forward. You deserve self-validation and self-approval. This will give you a sense of hope and give you the patience that you deserve to help you work through your losses.

I want you to be able to validate yourself so you can say:

> "Today someone asked my opinion and I had one. Yes, me! I—who have never felt safe forming my own opinion—I had one."
> "Today I got angry and I knew it. In the past it took me six years to figure out I had a feeling and another two years to know it was anger."
> "I didn't work through my whole lunch hour, just half of it."
> "Today I received a compliment. I said thank you and didn't say 'Yes, but....'"

Affirming, approving, validating—these are the little steps for which you deserve applause. It is very important to stop, take time to identify the little steps in recovery, the little bits of success. This strengthens your sense of self and reinforces your new beliefs. Also, try not to be preoccupied with what hasn't changed for you yet. Focus on what is happening now.

As a way of making self-validation a habit, take time out each day to focus on your positive attributes. Recognize at least three new behaviors or attitudes that are reflective of your real, valuable self and the new direction you are taking.

Another reason it is crucial to learn to validate yourself early in recovery is that, very quickly, you will be confronted with one of the most frightening issues of all, the need to give up some control.

LETTING GO OF SOME CONTROL

Most of us adults know a lot about the word control, but those of us raised in either chaotic or rigid environments know very little about the word *some*, S-O-M-E, as in "some control." To us, control has been something we either have or we don't. The concept of "some control" has seemed as impossible as being "a little bit pregnant."

Perceiving control to be an all-or-nothing experience, naturally we don't want to give it up. That would be the same, we believe, as being "out of control." Also, we don't want to give up control because it once protected us, so giving up control is frightening because it has been vital to our sense of safety. Control of the external forces in your environment is a survival mechanism. It may be self-protection in a physical sense. Or, from the standpoint of your beliefs and feelings, control is what allowed you, when you were a young child, to make sense out of your life.

Controlling behavior is an attempt to bring order and consistency into an inconsistent and unpredictable family situation. Controlling behavior is a defense against our shame. Feeling a sense of control gives children a sense of power at that time in our lives when we are overwhelmed with our powerlessness, helplessness, our fears. Giving up control as an adult is difficult, when up to this point in life it has been of great value.

One way children learn to control is by manipulating their environment. They try to control the aspects of their lives that are tangible or concrete. You can see this when children act as their own parent, maybe also as the parent to their brothers and sisters. Often, they act as a parent to their mother and father.

Susan said she actually used to discipline herself for having misbehaved. "I would do things and not be reprimanded. I talked back to my parents. I would swear. Maybe I would be late for school. So I would discipline myself. I put myself on restriction. I would role play verbal reprimands. I used television shows as my guide. I actually raised myself fairly well."

At eleven years of age, Tim was the one who set the bedtime for his younger brother and sister. He made sure they had a bath before they went to bed. He literally tucked them in himself. He then made sure their lunches were made before school the next morning.

Fourteen-year-old Kim used to call her father to tell him what he needed to do before he came home from work. This same youngster was the one who covered her mother up after she passed out on the couch, so that she wouldn't get too cold during the middle of the night.

Ten-year-old Paul put the car in the garage every night when his dad would leave it running in the middle of the front yard. He didn't want the neighbors to think there was anything wrong at his house.

These are examples of children trying their best to create order and safety in their lives.

While many children try to control that which is external—people, places, and things—children may also attempt to control internal, intangible aspects of their personal lives. Some children become very controlling by withholding their feelings. Discounting their feelings usually goes along with this.

> *"I'm not angry. What's there to be angry about? I've seen it before."*
> *"I wasn't embarrassed. I'm used to those things by now."*
> *"No, I didn't feel sad. Last time I cried, they called me names."*

Some children become very controlling by diminishing their own needs, not expecting anything, not asking for anything.

> *"I don't need to go to my friend's house. Who would be home to take care of my sister?"*
> *"I don't want a birthday party. Dad wouldn't show up anyway."*
> *"I don't want my mom to come to the PTA meeting. Last time she showed up, it was a major fiasco."*

Diminishing needs and withholding feelings are invisible, internal controlling mechanisms. This is self-control, protection to ward off further pain by repressing desires and feelings.

Some children become very controlling through withdrawal and isolation. They go off in the corner and read. They daydream in their bedroom or, when teenagers, spend as little time at home as possible. They establish a social boundary that says, "Stay away. I don't need you. I don't want you. Let me go do something alone in safety that keeps me from the depth of my painful feelings."

Because of their early experiences, people do differ in the depth of their control and in the ways they control. However, in my work, I have consistently observed some commonalities:

(1) The greater the physical and emotional chaos in a family, the greater a child will find the need for pervasive control.

(2) The faster the dysfunction in a family progresses and deepens, the less a child becomes an external controller and, instead, becomes more of an internal controller.

(3) When another family member is already an external controller, there is less need for another child to be an external controller, and so more often that child will learn to control internally only.

(4) External controllers also control internally, but some people are only internal controllers.

When we were children, whether internally or externally, our attempts to control were about survivorship. It made sense in the context of our environment, according to our child's logic.

Unfortunately, the continued need for control causes problems in our adult lives. We have spent years being hypervigilant, manipulating ourselves and others as a way of protection. Now, we literally don't know how to live life differently. We don't have any idea why we would want to live life differently. Our ways have been right, apparently, because we have survived.

Unfortunately, we have become so encapsulated and narrow in our view of the world, we don't see what others can so readily see—that we have become rigid, authoritarian, demanding, inflexible, and perfectionistic. We don't know how to listen. We cut people off in conversations and relationships. We don't ask for help. We can't see options. We have little spontaneity or creativity. We experience psychosomatic health problems. We intimidate people by withholding our feelings.

Blindly focused on our pursuit of safety, very often unaware of our emotional self, and yet so frightened and full of shame, we rely on what we know best—control. But the consequences are almost the opposite of what we had hoped for. Our needs do not get met. Our relationships are out of balance. Ultimately, our hypervigilance becomes burdensome and exhausting. Sadly, we don't know how to go about life any differently. In our confusion about what has gone wrong when we've tried so hard to make things right, we succumb to depression and/or resort to unhealthy ways to cope with sadness and pain.

While some people don't identify with having tried to be in control in their lives during their growing-up years, they will often speak of how strongly controlling one or both of their parents were, which indicates that the children were victims of control. When these young people grow up, they usually react in one of two ways. They may assume a victim position in adulthood. Or, most likely they will seek control in every area of life to make up for their loss, having grown up in the family loss environment which did not allow the children to develop a sense of personal power. These people are usually at least somewhat conscious of their efforts to have power and mastery over everything in life; they are usually blatantly angry, though they fail to acknowledge the anger. Their anger is also tightly controlled! Very often the anger that is felt began in direct response to a parent's controlling relationship.

Adults react to chronic parental control in many ways. For example, people with a food disorder are controlling what does and what does not go into their mouths, trying to compensate for the powerlessness they had over the abusive control they experienced. Another example can be seen when one person in a relationship dominates the other, as a result of the anger felt toward the highly controlling parent of the opposite sex. In other words, a woman would dominate her husband to act out her anger at her controlling father.

Whether or not we have sought control to make up for the lack of control in our lives, fear and shame are the factors that fuel our need to seek control.

Ways We Try To Control

People demonstrate control in a variety of ways, but the following four postures are particularly common ways people disguise their conscious or unconscious attempts to control:

(1) Sweet Controller*—This person is polite, pleasant, and sweet in order to get what she/he wants. We often respond positively to this person, attracted to her seeming innocence, or his charming smile, but in reflection we recognize all we know about them is how sweet they are. We realize we have become, often one more time, a part of a "one up/one down" relationship, and we are in the one down role.

(2) Distant Controller—This is the person who is rigidly efficient, emotionally cold, and who develops a sense of mastery by paying attention to detail. A person like this is great to have in your life when you need a "detail person," but is difficult to be close to.

(3) Passive Controller—This person is known to many as the martyr, as is reflected by the words, "I don't care. Do whatever *you* want. You are more important than I am. Anyway, it doesn't matter to me." The control attempt lies in the unspoken intent, "But I'll get you in the end!"

(4) Angry Controller—This person is an intimidator, who says to the world, "I want what I want, when I want it, and I will get it!"

What all controllers have in common is they operate from a basis of fear. Their fear has been so great that it has had led to their need to protect themselves by staying in control, and as a result, they have become disrespectful of other people's needs and others' boundaries. Ultimately, virtually all controllers will become angry. This is inevitable, because they are going through life unable to get their needs met.

As controllers, all that we know about is "all or nothing," "one or ten." We cannot see that almost nothing in real life is on a "one or ten" basis, but that nearly everything lies in a continuum between the numbers two through nine. So, our experience in life is that we are in total control—or we have just lost it! When we feel our tight

---

*Sweetness does not equate to being controlling. Sweetness is a wonderful virtue. But to use sweetness to cover a basis of fear, and to have a disrespect for other people's needs and boundaries are not the same thing as being genuinely sweet.

hold on control threatened, we scramble to regain control in any way we know. It feels like a life-or-death threat to lose it!

Yet, if we want to experience recovery, we must let go of some control. We must hear the word S-O-M-E. Control is not an "all or nothing" issue.

For those of you in Twelve Step programs, what I am saying in no way contradicts the First Step, which refers to the need to surrender, i.e., to give up control. What the First Step asks us to do is to give up trying to control what cannot be controlled. This is analogous to the Serenity Prayer:

God grant me the serenity
to accept the things I cannot change
the courage to change the things I can
and the wisdom to know the difference.

Willingness to give up control is vital to being willing to engage in the recovery process, but this is not something you learn to do all at once. Giving up control does not have to be an all-or-nothing process. As one gives up control, it is okay to practice giving up control in those areas that feel psychologically safe. You may begin to practice letting go of control more easily in one setting than another. You may begin by "letting go" of which store you shop in, of who chooses the movie you see with your partner or friend or, chooses which route you take on a trip. The more you practice "letting go," the easier it will become to begin gradually giving up control in the areas that cause the greatest pain, such as past loss conditions or present self-destructive behaviors.

Control Still Feels Like A Matter of Life And Death

Why are we so afraid of giving up control? We need to know what our belief is before we can challenge it and put it into perspective. For most of us, control still represents what it meant to us as children. If we grew up with chronic loss—the abandonment experiences and loss conditions—then "giving up control" is equated with "being out of control." When I ask adults what "out of control" meant to them as children, their answers include a wide range of painful memories:

—chaos, confusion
—being abandoned
—being left alone
—not being noticed
—being called names
—more anger, fear, sadness
—getting hit
—not being valued
—dying, death

Some people feared their or another's physical death. For others, it was emotional death and/or spiritual death, the death of their inner child's spirit.

While the above responses are perceptions of adults looking back on childhood, their beliefs are still there, below awareness, for those who have not yet dealt with this in recovery. You may be thirty-five years old, but when you experience loss of control it is experienced from the reference of being a child, i.e., your fear of chaos and confusion. Something bad is bound to happen—someone will be hit, be abandoned, or die.

Yet, as people so often remind me, those beliefs from childhood no longer make sense. "After all," you may be thinking, "an adult should be able to think things through, so such fears would be childish." My response is: Who is that speaking? Where does that internalized "should" message come from? Clearly, it is an echo from a long time ago. What is involved here is the emotional vulnerability a person carries from childhood.

We aren't conscious of these fears—these are internalized fears imprinted deep within our emotional beings that we have never been able to address. Now is the time to do so. We need to explore what control has meant and put it into its proper perspective.

The following chart, "A Continuum Of Control," offers a useful portrayal of the "amount" of control a family and the individual members live with on a continuum.

Continuum of Control
Control Issues In Rigid, Chaotic, and Healthy Families

1------------------2   3   4   5   6   7   8   9------------------10

No Control "1"	Some (S-O-M-E) Control "2 - 9"	Total Control "10"
Family of Origin:		
Chaotic; extreme disorder. Rigid controls attempted to create some safety	"Normal." Some order; some disorder. control not a central family issue	Rigidity; no apparent disorder. Hidden feelings grow chaotic, threaten to emerge, trigger chaotic events
Abandonment experiences	Few, if any abandonment experiences	Abandonment experiences
"All or nothing" thinking	Life is neither "all or nothing"	"All or nothing" thinking
Survival dependent on following family rules superimposed on chaos to create appearance of order	Survival or parental approval not dependent on family rules	Parental approval and protection dependent on following family rules prohibiting natural disorder
Family rules; Don't talk, Don't trust, Don't feel	Family behaviors: Talk. Trust. Feel	Family rules; Don't talk, Don't trust. Don't feel
Belief: Life is unmanageable	Belief: Some things in life can be managed; some cannot	Belief: Life is a matter to be managed
In Adult Life:		
Fear of loss of control of self, feelings	Loss of control not central fear. Confident and accepting of self and feelings	Fear of loss of control of self, feelings
Fear of being abandoned by loved ones	Not driven by fear of abandonment. Trust in self & others	Fear of being abandoned by loved ones
Attempts to control based on past beliefs, feelings, and behaviors or to act out chaos	Recognition of where you have the power to affect things and where you don't	Attempts to control based on past beliefs, feelings, and behaviors or to reject all control
External approval sought for beliefs and behaviors	Internal reference for feelings, behaviors, and beliefs	External approval sought for beliefs and behaviors
Poor Inner Adult recovery skills	Activated Inner Adult skills: Validate self, "let go" control, feel feelings, identify needs, set limits and boundaries	Poor Inner Adult recovery skills

An Exercise In Relaxing About Control

Because the whole notion of control is so important, it may help you to take time to focus on what control symbolizes for you. Slowly and gently read the following thoughts:

Sit back in a comfortable seat and relax....Breathe deeply....Uncross your legs and arms....Gently close your eyes and reflect back in time to your growing-up years.

Recognizing how you exerted control externally or internally, finish this sentence:

Giving up control in my family would have meant.........
Giving up control in my family would have meant.........
Giving up control in my family would have meant.........
Giving up control in my family would have meant.........
Giving up control in my family would have meant.........

If you have difficulty with this exercise, another way to benefit from it is to describe the controlling behavior (remember, controlling behavior was developed to protect you, so don't be judgmental). For example:

Not taking care of my mother would have meant......
or
Not doing the grocery shopping would have meant......
or
Not holding in my feelings would have meant......

Repeating these sentences allows you to access a deeper level of honesty. Now ask yourself if control means the same thing to you today. Where does the concept of *some control* fit into your beliefs and your feelings right now?

Letting go of our old beliefs of what giving up control will mean and integrating the words *some control* into our lives, we will be able to internalize, in time, the knowledge that it is in letting go of the need to be in control that we experience—

—peace, serenity
—relaxation
—ability to listen to others
—ability to listen to ourselves
—trust in ourselves
—lack of fear
—spontaneity
—creativity
—fun, play
—energy
—our present feelings
—intimacy with others

As much as we become aware of the frightening connotation that the issue of control has for us, it is now equally as important to remind ourselves of the positive aspects for ourselves and our lives that come with not needing to stay in control. It is in giving up some control we genuinely become empowered. The above list reminds us of why we are doing our recovery work. There truly are rewards.

FEELING YOUR FEELINGS

In the process of exploring the issue of control, we quickly become aware of our feelings. And we have so much to feel about. People will have feelings around every recovery issue. Without exploring and becoming more comfortable with your emotional self, you will quickly become stuck in the process. With each feeling there are three areas that need to be looked at:

(1) Fear of the feeling
(2) Identification of the feeling
(3) Expression of the feeling

While many adults are fearful of feelings, incapable of identifying any feelings, other people are very clear about what it is they feel. Usually though, that is when there is only one dominant emotion. Some people may walk through life and the only feeling they know is their anger, or for another the only feeling they know is their sadness. Others will know their fear or their helplessness. There are some people who "only love life." They are never angry, sad, frightened. They are always accepting, loving, and understanding.

We would all like life to be so wonderful! To make lemonade out of a lemon is wonderful, but to refuse to acknowledge the lemon ever existed is denial—denial of ourselves and our experiences. I believe it is when we can own and accept our present feelings, whether they are irritations, fears, sadnesses, joys, etc., that we are able to love life. We want to be able to access a whole range of feelings. A part of recovery is learning to identify a range of feelings and then learn the appropriate expression of those feelings.

Although no parents can be perfect role models, the role modeling we saw in our dysfunctional home was seriously distorted. Our models for expressing feelings were people who denied feelings, contradicted our perception of reality, and generally could not express positive or negative feelings in healthy ways.

We saw people rage in anger or consistently walk away in silence, succumbing to fear and helplessness. Many of our parents converted one feeling to another, i.e., they became sad when angry and visa versa. They added further confusion when they told us we had nothing to be frightened of when we did. They told us we had no right to be angry, but that we should feel grateful.

We wanted so much to love our parents totally, without reservation. Then something would happen. They would act in such hurtful ways, we couldn't totally love them, leaving us confused and feeling guilty. As a result of living with a distorted and twisted expression of feelings, we watched, learned, and repeated the same pattern.

Before you can express certain feelings, you need to face your fears about what might happen if you do. In other words, what are you afraid might happen if, for example, you express hate for your mother, or if you start to cry because your father left you? Typically, some of those fears are (1) you won't like me; (2) you are going to be able to see how bad I really am; (3) you are going to perceive me as weak; (4) you are going to perceive me as vulnerable, and to me that is the same thing as being bad; (5) you are going to tell me that I have no reason for feeling this way; or (6) I will not be in control and that is not okay.

These fears were most likely valid for you at one time in your life. When you expressed an honest emotion, your parents and other caretakers may have responded with some kind of rejection, which felt like abandonment. We need to ask ourselves, "Is that still true today?" Sometimes we never ask and yet we operate on fears that are ten, twenty, or even many more years old.

If these fears are true today, that is, if we express our feelings in the presence of certain people and their response is negative, now we know we have a choice to make. Do we want to believe that other person's judgment? Or do we want to validate ourselves, relying on our own internal judgment and strengthening our core of positive self-regard? For a while, we will feel anxious about these choices, so we need to confront these fears early in recovery to allow ourselves to be honest about who we are.

You may also have difficulty expressing feelings because you have difficulty identifying them. If so, you need to go back and work on learning to identify feelings. People from family systems that did not sanction the expression of feelings may honestly have difficulty recognizing that their clenched fists are signs of anger. Some people have had tears stream down their face and have not recognized their own sadness.

Early in the process of exploring feelings, it is not uncommon to ask people how they are feeling and hear the reply, "I don't know." Many therapists perceive that response as resistance. However, it is my experience that the person probably doesn't know. This is known as psychic numbness, emotional anesthesia, or frozen feelings.

If you are able to identify your feelings and still not express them, that is often due to the fear of what would happen. In this case, your fear needs to be explored further to find the freedom to use your emotional skills.

To summarize, if you find yourself stuck in the area of feelings, you need to assess the problem to see if it has to do with the (1) fear of feeling; (2) identification of the feeling; or (3) expression of the feeling. Remember, do not confuse doing your grief work with the issue of exploring feelings in general. Identifying obstacles in dealing with your feelings will help you develop the skills to do the grief work. And, at the same time, it will give you the skills to express your feelings in the present.

Feelings are cues and signals that tell us that we have a need. If we pay attention to the feeling, we can learn what it is that we need. So, if you feel some discomfort, and reflect on what you are feeling, you will then identify the feeling—loneliness, for example. Knowing when you are lonely is important, and you can deal with that in the present. But if you do not listen and respectfully respond to the feeling, you may try to compensate with some counterproductive behaviors instead, such as overwork or overeating.

It is also helpful to know how you have become accustomed to compensating for your feelings, because those compensatory behaviors are also cues that tell us what we are feeling and what we need. For instance, to recognize overeating as a cover-up for sadness, helps you to identify an opportunity to change your feeling response. Many, many people run from their feelings with certain behaviors. Some people use work, exercise, or shopping to distract themselves. Others use food or alcohol to medicate.

Feelings are also indicators that help us set boundaries that provide safety for us. Expressing our feelings allows us to connect and bond with others. This is what allows us to experience intimacy. Our emotional self is significant and vital to the opportunity to experience meaning in life. Yet, that does not mean that health is about sharing outwardly every feeling we experience. A sign of recovery is the ability to know what you feel when you feel it, to be comfortable with your emotional self, and then to be able to determine whether or not and with whom you share feelings.

IDENTIFYING YOUR NEEDS

Learning to identify our feelings accesses our ability to recognize our needs. In families marked by chronic loss, children's needs are not met. Adults don't focus on the children's needs and the children don't or can't, because they are too young and without adequate adult support and nurture. And, as we've said, often the children were kept busy taking care of others.

For many of us, this focus on others became a safety net, a part of our identity, and has carried over into our adult lives. The pay off is, "If I don't focus on me, I don't feel the depth of my helplessness and powerlessness." But, as a result of not knowing our needs, they don't get met. No wonder we are depressed, angry, or confused. "Me? Oh, I don't have any needs. No, I don't need anything." *Needs* is spoken as if it is a foreign word, or even a vulgar word for many of us.

Taking a look at your needs can be as frightening as the idea of looking at your control issues. Before you are going to be able to actively wrestle with the concept of having needs, you will have to let go of some control. You will have to have a strong sense of what your feelings are, because your feelings are cues and signals that are needed to help identify needs. You are going to have to believe more in your own worth and that you deserve to have your needs met.

It is easy for people to get caught up in the semantics of the word "needs." In grade school we were taught we only have five basic needs—air, food, clothing, shelter and water—and everything else is a "want." This was presented as the basis for physical survival. The life you are now rebuilding is not only about physical existence; it is about going beyond. Our psychological, emotional, social, and spiritual needs are that which give meaning to life.

When needs are attended to, children learn skills that allow them to grow emotionally and psychologically, that allow them to move into adulthood with a sense of belonging, a sense of value, and a sense of competence. While your needs may not have been met as a child, you have an opportunity to meet your needs now. A major part of recovery is taking responsibility for meeting your needs. Regardless of your original parenting, it is no longer going to be your mother or father who will meet your needs. You will need to take responsibility, you will meet those needs for yourself.

If your needs include establishing new relationships, it will mean finding people in your adult life today who are in a position to respond to you. This is about reparenting the child that is still within you.

Because many of us were given strong reinforcement for diminishing and not looking at their own needs, we need to confront the concept of selfishness. "Is it okay for my needs to be important?" "Is it okay for my needs to be more important to me than other people's needs at this particular time?"

Forty-four-year old Ellen, daughter of two alcoholic parents, married to her third alcoholic husband, was in a counseling session. When she was asked, "What do you need?" Ellen looked at the therapist, confused. She then looked away as if she had answered the question and was ready to move on. The therapist said, "Ellen, you have been taking care of other people all of your life. You took care of your parents, three husbands, and two children. It is time to take care of you. What do you need?"

Ellen, clearly agitated, looked quickly away as if looking for the door. It was obvious she wanted to change the subject. Once again, the therapist said, "Ellen, Ellen, what do you need? Not anyone else, but you." This time Ellen's eyes opened wide and her body began to jerk, her knees jerked up and down; her head jerked slightly back, as if she were going to convulse. Being frightened, the therapist reached out, grabbing Ellen where she was twitching the most, at the knee and shoulder. As she was touching Ellen, she very calmly, yet firmly spoke to Ellen, saying, "Ellen, it is over. It is all over. You don't have to take care of anyone else. You only have to take care of you."

The twitching subsided. The therapist, holding onto Ellen, now purposely pushed the obviously very loaded issue: "Ellen, what do you need?" Quietly, Ellen responded, "Need? What do I need? When has it ever been safe for me to ask myself what it is I need?"

It had never been safe for Ellen to consider her needs. Her priority had always been feeling a sense of responsibility for others who were not taking responsibility for themselves. Now, it would be important for Ellen to recognize her own needs as an adult in order for them to be met. But, before she would be able to do that effectively, she would need to take a look at the what the issue of "having needs" had meant her entire life, beginning with her growing-up years.

While many adults like Ellen don't recognize they have needs, many others compartmentalize their needs, rejecting those needs that would involve others. This is the case when someone operates from the attitude, "I don't need you. I don't need them. I'm doing just fine all by myself." This attitude of rigid self-sufficiency is a determined stance to not be hurt or rejected by another.

Lynne, at age thirty-five, was extremely capable. While she allowed herself to get married, she didn't allow herself any interdependency. "I take responsibility for all of my needs. I always have. I never trusted that I would be heard, so I didn't share my desires, my wants. It wasn't that Tom wouldn't have been there for me—I just didn't give him a chance. I was so used to not trusting anyone would be there for me or follow through with their promises, it didn't dawn on me to ask others to be there. After all, I became an expert at taking care of myself."

Unfortunately, this dynamic became a major source of discord in Lynne's marriage. She and Tom were not able to achieve the intimacy Tom wanted, and he ultimately chose to leave the marriage. Lynne stayed out of any committed relationships for the next twelve years. Looking at her issues of trust, fear of rejection, and fear of asking others to be there for her needs is her focus in recovery today. It is Lynne's hope that she will have the intimacy she deserves.

Identifying Now What You Needed As A Child

To become more skilled at recognizing your needs as an adult, you have to be empathetic to your childhood needs. Because your needs today are often the same as when you were a child, discounting your past needs only serves to detract from believing that you have a right to meet your needs as an adult.

In working with clients, I have found that for adults to identify their unmet needs as children, it is very helpful for them to go through an exercise of writing a letter to their parents. This exercise also leads them to see that those childhood needs are often their needs today. This letter will never be mailed, read to, or given to that parent. The purpose is not to retaliate, blame, or hurt the parent. The purpose is to facilitate the grief process and identify needs.

To write this letter, begin by thanking your parent for whatever positive things he or she gave you. Then, tell this person what you needed that you didn't get.

Here is an example of this exercise. It is a letter written by a thirty-three-year old woman:

Dear Dad,

I want to thank you for some things when I was young. I am glad you told me you loved me. I believed it. I always liked it when we played.

But, Dad, there was so much I needed that I just didn't get. You became so tyrannical, so controlling, and so dishonest. More than anything, I needed you to let me be a kid, to let me make mistakes. I lived in fear of not being perfect for you. By being perfect in your image, I gave up my childhood. I needed to play, Dad. I needed to be me and not just a part of your self-image.

I needed you to be nicer to Mom. You never remembered her birthday, or bought her a Christmas present. Because you drank, she was always at work. I needed to know her better.

As a teenager, I hated the fact I was so fearful of you. I was scared, terrified all the time. I hated how I felt sexually. I felt so dirty because of your attitude about me and boys. I always felt ashamed. The funny part, Dad, is I wasn't sexually active.

I needed to eat dinner as a family. We ate anywhere from 7:30 at night until 11:30. There was nothing ever pleasant about dinner. You didn't even eat half the time.

You know what, Dad—I still need you.

This letter elicits many powerful feelings. This is the kind of letter that helps to move you through the grief process and at the same time helps you become empathetic to your own plight a child. It also allows you to see how your childhood needs are often carried into adulthood. After writing a letter like this, read it out loud (not to the directed person). There is usually as much power and value in the reading as there was in writing it.

In the above letter, this woman identified her childhood needs as:

(1) I needed to be a kid.

(2) I needed to play.

(3) I needed to make mistakes.

(4) I needed to be me, not you.

(5) I needed to know Mom better.

(6) I needed to feel comfortable with my sexuality.

(7) I needed healthy rituals.

(8) I needed you, Dad.

By identifying these childhood needs, the writer identifies her present-day needs. These aren't needs that her parent will meet today, but they are still present-day needs, irrespective of age. An exercise like this says:

(1) I need to play, to discover my spontaneity, frivolity, creativity.

(2) I need to feel I am of value even though I make mistakes.

(3) I need to discover who I am, separate from my father's needs of me.

(4) I need to know my mother better.

(5) I need to feel comfortable with my sexuality.

(6) I need healthy rituals.

(7) I need my father.

This woman at thirty-three, or at any age, can still work on these needs. Of course, her parents may not be available or accessible, but owning the need is the first step to coming to terms with it.

I encourage you, the reader, to take time to write a similar letter.

Choose a person from whom you have experienced loss. After the salutation, Dear _____, begin by thanking that person for what he or she has given you. Then tell the person what it was you needed that you didn't get. When you get ready to write, with pencil in hand, just begin—don't try to plan or think ahead about what you want to say. Don't be preoccupied with writing form or style. What you say is what is important here, not how well you write.

When you have completed your letter, read it aloud. This process brings relief as stored feelings are identified and released. After reading your letter and having time to be with your feelings, go back to your letter and circle the needs you have expressed. The needs you identified in your childhood will give you a focus and direction for needs you can still attend to today.

Valuing needs as normal and human allows us to be more open to recognizing our needs. If you have difficulty focusing on yourself, if you also feel empty, depressed, possibly victimized, or angry, repeatedly ask yourself, "What do *I* need? What do *I* want? What do *I* need? What do *I* want?"

As you let go of control and feel your feelings, your needs will become more evident. As you continue to practice self-validation, you will have a stronger belief that you deserve to have those needs met.

It is in knowing what your needs are that they are most apt to be met.

SETTING LIMITS AND BOUNDARIES

When you begin to meet your needs, it leads you to the next skill, which is setting limits and boundaries. Being raised in troubled families meant that our boundaries as children were not respected, often not even recognized. Or we may have lived with rigid, walled boundaries, offering no opportunity for any emotional or spiritual connection. Unhealthy boundaries create confusion about who is responsible for what, adding to more distortion about guilt and shame. As a result of living with chronic boundary violation/distortion, we are often either not skilled in setting boundaries or we are disrespectful and intrusive of others' boundaries.

A boundary is a limit or edge that defines you as separate from others—a separate human being, not someone else's possession. For each of us, our skin marks the limit of our physical self. We have other boundaries as well. We have limits to what is psychologically and physically safe. We have emotional, spiritual, sexual, relationship, and intellectual boundaries.

Emotional boundaries define the self, our ideas, feelings, and values. We set emotional boundaries by choosing how we let people treat us. Our spiritual development comes from our inner self. Only we know the spiritual path for ourselves. We have sexual boundaries, limits on what is safe and appropriate sexual behavior. We have a choice about who we interact with sexually and the extent of that interaction. We have relationship boundaries. The roles we play define the limits of appropriate interaction with others. Our intellectual boundaries offer us the opportunity to enjoy learning and teaching. They allow us to be curious and inspired.

Because we were raised with unhealthy boundaries, we often normalize hurtful behavior and can't recognize boundary distortion. The following are various types of boundary violation.

Emotional:
    feelings denied
    told what we can and cannot feel
    being raged at
    criticism
    being belittled
    lack of expectations
    being terrorized
Spiritual:
    going against personal values or rights to please others
    taught to believe in a hurtful higher power
    no spiritual guidance
    no sense of prayer or gratitude

Sexual:
>   being sexual for partner, not self
>   lack of sexual information during puberty
>   given misinformation about our bodies, our development
>   shame for being wrong sex
>   exposure to pornography
>   sexualized comments
>   all forms of sexual abuse

Relationship:
>   falling in love with anyone who reaches out
>   allowing someone to take as much as they can from you
>   letting others define your reality
>   believing others can anticipate your needs

Intellectual:
>   denied information
>   not allowed to make mistakes
>   not encouraged to question
>   being called stupid
>   encouraged to follow a parent's dream rather than your own

Physical:
>   accepting touch you do not want
>   not taught appropriate hygiene
>   violence, pushing, shoving, kicking, pinching, excessive tick-
>   ling
>   hitting
>   touch deprivation

Before we can establish healthy boundaries, it is helpful to the process to identify boundary violations in your life. Think about significant people in your growing up years and reflect on the six areas of boundaries with each person. Note (1) healthy boundaries and (2) unhealthy boundaries that were experienced.

Repeat this same exercise with the significant people in your life today. Once identified, you are in a better position to re-define your boundaries for a healthier self. Healthy boundaries are flexible enough that we can choose what to let in and what to keep out. We cannot maintain boundaries without the ability to know our feelings. Feelings are our signals to comfort, safety, discomfort, danger.

We want to have boundaries that are flexible but with limits; they move appropriately in response to situations, out for strangers, in for those we are intimate with. They should be distinct enough to preserve our individual self, yet open to new ideas. They are firm to maintain values and priorities, open to communicate our priorities. Boundaries tell us that certain behaviors are inappropriate in the context of certain relationships. A healthy boundary protects without isolating, contains without imprisoning.

Our ability to protect ourselves psychologically and physically is related to the strength of our boundaries. Boundaries bring order to our lives. As we strengthen our boundaries, we gain a clearer sense of ourselves and our relationship to others. They empower us to determine how we'll be treated by others.

Establishing healthy boundaries is vital to recovery, to getting needs met, to developing a sense of self, and all of this leads to being strong enough to be able to separate yourself from past shameful messages and behaviors—and no longer internalizing shame.

Developing boundaries is knowing your physical and psychological comfort zone, or safety zone, knowing what you like and don't like. It is having enough of a sense of your own self separate from others. It is a part of defining who you are.

In recovery, you need to ask yourself what it is you want. What do you need? What do you desire? One establishes boundaries that allow those things to be. Limit setting is the skill that allows one to maintain boundaries. In order to protect boundaries, in order for them to remain intact and useful, you need to know your feelings. Feelings are cues and signals to whether those boundaries are being respected. As well, one must believe their needs are important to be able to define boundaries.

Fear of other's rejection, the need for approval, and fear of anger are major stumbling blocks to defining boundaries and a willingness to set limits. Should you believe you have done the work you need to do to be better skilled in establishing boundaries, but are nonetheless stuck, go back and address these three stumbling blocks.

The skills to be able to set limits and establish boundaries take you to another issue, and that is the ability to say no and yes. By establishing boundaries and setting limits, we begin to use the words no and yes with freedom. For so many of us, it was not safe to say no as a child. Without the freedom to say no, yes was said with tremendous fear and helplessness or out of a desperate need for approval and love. Others of us grew up in families where 'no' meant 'yes' and today we cannot hear people's 'no's.

There is often pain and confusion around how no and yes were offered in troubled families. That pain needs to be acknowledged. As with the other foundational issues, you will need to apply the four steps to no and yes in your life.

A part of recovery will mean talking about the many times you couldn't say no but wanted to (and all the times you said yes, out of fear), and the anger and the pain that goes with that. In recovery you will recognize that no can be a word that acts as a friend to protect you. It offers you choice. In recovery we need to acknowledge the times we heard yes when we needed to hear no. In doing so it will allow us to be more sensitive to others' boundaries. We all have the power and right to say no and yes. It is my hope that yes is a right that is offered freely, rather than out of fear or the need for approval, and that when we say no we are actually saying yes to ourselves.

CREATING A CORE OF STRENGTH WITH THE RECOVERY SKILLS

As you learn to validate yourself, to let go of some control—knowing that doesn't not mean being out of control—and to begin feeling your true feelings, and identify your needs as well as set limits and boundaries for yourself—as you learn these new skills and practice them, you create an inner core of strength that allows you to move forward with growing confidence. These skills will offer you a foundation to go further in recovery and address more complex issues of loss, abandonment, and shame.

You will be developing a true inner sense of self that will allow you to discover new choices and bring meaning into life. These skills will help you develop a more solid sense of self. You will no longer just be a reactor; instead, you will act on your own beliefs and decisions. You will no longer be propelled by fear or shame, but you will have a more solid belief in what you value, what you want, and a much more gracious, supportive, and forgiving attitude toward yourself.

Life will no longer be viewed through a lens of fear or doubt. You will rightfully expect more from life and feel hopeful. The foundation has been laid for you to continue addressing those areas important to you.

TURNING POINT:

Learning to love yourself does not mean you love others less.

Instead, it frees you to love them more.

5
The House We Lived In

No More Roles, No More Secrets

"What if we thought of the family less as the determining influence by which we are formed and more the raw material from which you make a life."
— Thomas Moore, *Care of the Soul*

"When our worth and our identity are no longer defined by a survival role, we have choices about meeting our own needs and developing in our own ways that we did not have before."

— Claudia Black

A family is like a house with many rooms. Picture the family you grew up in as one room in the framework of this very large house. The family you have now, as an adult, is the central living area, in fact, the "family room." Each of the other, different rooms of the house represents the previous generations of families and newly created ones, all of which are connected directly or indirectly. Through the doors to those rooms pass family secrets, family stories, and beliefs about what is and isn't true, and what a person should and shouldn't do.

In this chapter, we'll explore our family home, the family secrets, and family stories. Then, in chapter 6, we'll look at the new choices for our relationships, new ways of acting and reacting that not only strengthen our personal freedom, but also create greater intimacy with the people we love. As you begin these new ways of interacting, however, there will be some uneasiness and upsetting feelings, maybe difficult times; for in several ways, you are exchanging the role you have played for many years in return for a new way of being and relating.

RECASTING YOUR ROLE

Often there is an awkwardness that comes with recasting your role in the family—that is, changing your beliefs and changing the behavior role you adapted to play according to the family rules. In family relationships, every change you make affects someone else. What you are doing is, in essence, changing the family script, the family story that so often has been passed down generations. These changes not only feel awkward, but also very scary, especially to those who have not actively chosen to take an open look at their family dynamics and history.

Also, other family members will very likely be confused by your changes. They may resist your new attitudes and skills. Even though most of us, because of the bonds developed in our early years, choose to maintain some type of relationship with our parents and siblings, this is often difficult when you are seeking personal change and other family members are not.

As we attend to our childhood issues, as we lessen our denial, we discover our true selves, and we uncover family secrets. This is very frightening to family members who have spent years protecting themselves, and possibly others, from the pain of the truth. Recovery means letting go of the secrets.

FAMILY SECRETS

Secrets are handed down from one generation to another. Secrets are pieces of information that are withheld from others often out of shame, and many times with the intent to protect someone, yourself or another.

Paul discovered a secret his mother had kept after she died. Her parents had been from Austria, not Switzerland as he had been told. Because of fear of religious persecution, they had changed their name and even the facts about who they were and where they had come from.

In Merle's case, her mother consciously chose not to tell her that she might carry a physically disabling terminal illness to any male children. Afraid that no man would want to marry Merle, her mother thought if her daughter never knew, she would not be limited in her marriage options. In time, Merle had many suitors and did marry, but she also bore a child who died young from this transgenerational illness. The mother's concerns were sincere and out of love, but in trying to protect her daughter as she did, she denied Merle the chance to make important decisions for herself.

As is often the case, the intent of the secret was to protect. While both Paul and Merle understood their parents' concerns, Paul was not able to share a piece of history that, for him, created pain. He didn't have the opportunity to assist in lessening his mother's shame as he would have liked. He lost an opportunity for a significant intimate passage. As a result of her lack of information, Merle would experience the consequences of a decision her parents made for her, a decision which undermined the possibility of choice.

The Power Of Secrets

Secrets are powerful because they can control you. Very often, the primary problem of a secret is not the content of the secret itself, but what you must do to keep the secret information out of sight. In a family, it is the proverbial skeleton in the closet, and everyone in the family is held responsible to remain on guard in case someone outside the family gets too near the closet door.

Whether secrets are passed down unbeknown to others or people actively collude to hide the information, it is fair to say that as a young child, you had no choice in the matter; you were more or less coerced to keep the family secret. As an adult, however, you are now enforcing the secrecy on yourself. You may not be aware of it, but truly, you are the one making the choice to keep certain information away from prying eyes. The secret is just that—only information—and the choice is yours to tell it, to admit it, or to keep it hidden.

By admitting the reality of what is, you deflate the power of the secret. You can't drink away, or exercise away, eat away, work away, or through any other effort rationalize away the power of the secret. The only way is to end denial, to admit, to open the closet door—that is the only way to get free.

The awareness that now you can choose to be free from the secret is a turning point.

Living In The Shadow

Being raised in a shame-based family means being raised in a family where there is a pervasive need to deny that family secrets exist. The content of the secrets may be especially fearful, seem especially awful, or the adult secret-keepers may be especially rigid about the need to keep up appearances. Whatever the reason, all family life goes on as if under a dark cloud, because denial blocks the light of truth and shame grows rampant in the shadow.

Paul's and Merle's mothers were the self-appointed, lonely guardians of the family secret, but some of us were raised in families where secrets were blatantly shared. In Tim's case, he reflects, "My dad had to go to the psychiatric hospital periodically. He was manic depressive. We know that now, but we didn't know it when I was a child. Each time he went, all of us kids were told not to tell anyone, but if someone asked where he had gone, we were supposed to say he had to go back East to see a sick relative."

Cyndy remembers that "my older sister became pregnant twice, and each time we made up a lie for where she went for the last few months of her pregnancy. As soon as the lie was created, we were to never talk about her being 'gone' again."

These are secrets that the family members actively collude in. Yet, many of us live with secrets we don't even recognize. We may have lived with the secrecy of alcoholism without knowing it for what it was. Robin said, "I thought my dad was just crazy. He was forever a different personality. I knew he drank a lot, but so did lots of other people we knew. I didn't know he was addicted."

When we keep secrets, we become adept at rationalizing and

tolerating inappropriate behavior. As Tom said, "I thought I came from a normal family. But it was only after three years of being sober that I started to take a look at most things in my life. I began to see that it's not normal for parents to make their children drink from a toilet because they are caught playing in it. It is not normal for parents to create 'beating circles' with their children to discover which one did something wrong."

In circumstances like Tom's, there was no overt attempt to maintain secrets. Instead, there was a climate of secrecy about what occurred within the family. Pain was inflicted on purpose, but the children knew nothing different, having no other experience with being a family. Common to so many shame-based families is the phenomenon of not knowing what "normal" is. Everyone learns to tolerate inappropriate behavior. With the Don't Talk rule strongly intact, and no other role models to see due to the family's isolation, all the family members are subject to ongoing hurtful behavior.

When we experience something in life that we don't have the language for, we literally can't talk about it, and so the experience remains a secret. For example, some children don't identify their being abused because they are taught that physical abuse means being punched or slapped. They don't recognize that having their hair pulled can be abusive. They don't recognize that being slammed up against the wall is abuse. Also, they may believe a certain behavior has to happen every day, so when it only happens once a month, they rationalize it and so it remains a secret.

Anytime we do not have support within the family for our feelings, we learn to deny the pain and to create defenses that protect our vulnerable self. In time, we normalize painful experiences. "It only happened once." Or, "He didn't mean it." There is a need to deny and to protect ourselves when we don't have the external protection from other family members that we need in order to survive. When that happens, we end up keeping secrets and not even recognizing the secrets are there.

For some people the word *secret* implies an accompanying negative judgment. They believe that if the secret were known, they would be judged as damaged goods, as "less than" or "not as good as" others. Naturally, it is difficult for people with this belief to open up and admit their reality.

How can you tell if you are living with a secret? One way is to ask yourself, "Is there something about me or about my family that causes me to fear, if the truth were known to others, I would be rejected as their lover, friend, or employee?" Another way of asking is, "Is there something I cannot tell anyone because I am afraid of a negative reaction?" When you feel an implied threat associated with divulging some certain knowledge, this is information that restricts your life.

The Origins Of Secrets

What secrets did you grow up with? Were these secrets you were aware of at the time, or secrets you suspected then, and were confirmed later?

Secrets are often about embarrassing illnesses or problems with the law, such as being convicted of a crime or being in prison. Other problems occur in situations where family members have had extramarital affairs, pregnancies outside of marriage, abortions, addictions, or are involved in physical or sexual abuse.

What secrets do you have as an individual? There may even be some things only you know. Tom said he stole as a child and even now steals little things from friends and family. As far as he knows, no one knows that. Jeane said she was raped and no one else ever knew. Many women who have been raped have kept that experience and all of the many associated feelings a secret. Sally kept the knowledge of an unwanted pregnancy and miscarriage from her own husband.

Some of us have secret fears, such as "What if I lose my mind like my mother did?" Other fears might be, "I'm afraid my marriage is about to end," or "I am questioning my sexual orientation."

As we keep our secrets and carry the burden of hiding the information, guilt feelings often intensify and fear of discovery escalates. Fear causes pain, and too much pain often pushes us into seeking some self-destructive means of temporary pain relief. People keeping the secret of being sexually abused are commonly known to medicate their pain with alcohol, pills, or other drugs. Many people isolate themselves socially so they don't have to spend energy focused on what they "can't say." It is common to see someone in addiction recovery have a relapse when he or she feels extreme guilt or fear of discovery if a secret seems too frightening not to keep.

When we carry secrets, our view of the world is distorted. We are forever in a defensive position with others because we are always on the alert to protect our privacy. Trying to somehow distance ourselves from this "hidden information," we rationalize, distort, and repress the information in a way that blocks us from opportunities for emotional growth and precludes intimacy. Phyllis, for example, didn't want her new boyfriend to get close to her family, because she didn't want him to know certain things about them, such as her mother's addiction to pills or her brother's chronic abuse of cocaine. As a result, she would spend energy trying to stay separated from a significant part of her life. By not sharing the history of being sexually abused, Marie maintained a barrier between her partner and her that directly contributed to the sexual difficulties they were having as a couple.

When we have lived a life of withholding, when we have lived a life of secrecy, after a while it just no longer occurs to us to share with and confide in others. When we haven't talked about something for five, ten, or even thirty years, it doesn't occur to us to talk about it today. We have had years of training in being closed, protective, and secretive, so when things occur in the present that create fear, guilt, or shame, it is even less likely that we would choose to share. And the longer we hold in those old experiences, the more our shame is fueled and the more we act it out.

Out Of The Shadows, Out Of The Shame

Recovery is living a life free from shame. It is recognizing that you are not your secret; you are not your family secrets. You are a person with a myriad of experiences, some of them very painful. But, the pain of exposing the secret very, very rarely compares to the pain of keeping the secret. And, once the shameful knowledge is shared, the relief feels like the warmth of the summer sun after a very long, cold winter.

The following are some of the reasons people reveal secrets:

1. It relieves a burden. You no longer have to continue to lie to others. The secret has made life more difficult. It is no longer necessary to spend any more energy keeping it. Tony found that he felt great relief when he told his parents, twelve years after the fact, that he was the one, not his brother, who was driving the car when they had the wreck where another passenger was seriously injured.

2. It allows you to be true to yourself. It allows you to be honest with yourself. By telling the truth, Tony didn't have to suffer guilt every time he lied about his car wreck. When he could answer, "I was the driver," he could validate himself for making a mistake, but having the courage to admit it.

3. It prevents a possible surprise discovery. Some secrets are shared to lessen the shock or surprise that would be created if a significant other inadvertently found out. In fourteen years of marriage, John had not told his wife he had fathered a child sixteen years earlier. After this long time, John found tremendous relief knowing that even though it might be painful for his wife to learn he had a daughter, and that he had kept the knowledge hidden all these years, it would be better for her to know now, instead of some future day when the daughter appeared on their doorstep.

4. It enables you to have a more honest relationship with another. When you share a secret with someone, you are conveying the added message that you trust them with what is very important to you. You are often sharing at a more vulnerable level, and that often creates reciprocal willingness to be open and vulnerable on their part. The result is that a greater trust develops between the two of you.

5. It stimulates family change. When you decide to speak up, other family members are encouraged to make changes in their own lives. By telling your brothers and sisters that your mother has a drinking problem (that all of you have been the witness to, but have ignored) you are taking the first step in breaking everyone's denial. Potentially, this could result in everyone receiving help, including your mother. By telling of your sexual abuse, you may set an example that will inspire other family members who have been abused to speak up.

6. It could be a plea for help. When the secret you confide still needs to be attended to, e.g., if you are drinking too much and not yet in recovery, telling another person is a way for you to begin to move yourself toward getting help. If you were raped, telling someone, even many years later, may be your cry for help with unresolved grief and rage.

Secrets Become Confidences Shared With Safe People

As you create new ways of relating to the people in your family, it will be important for you not to play a part in the secrecy they may still want to maintain. Recovery does not include secrecy. It means speaking your truth. You, now in recovery, must end the Don't Talk rule for yourself. However, putting an end to secrecy does not mean that all things are to be shared with all people. Some events are very personal, and you will not want to share them with just anybody. In recovery, the word *secret* dissipates, and the word *confidence* replaces it, as you choose safe places and safe people to share with.

As you consider who you want to share your secrets with, you need to examine *why* you want to tell them. Sometimes people share secrets not to help themselves, but to hurt others. Some people share a secret for the pure act of revenge. "You have hurt me, so I will hurt you with this! Did you know that Dad isn't your real father!?" Any time anyone considers telling some powerful and potentially hurtful information, it is necessary to look at the motivation. You could rationalize that the other person has the right to know. Yes, they do. But are you the one to tell them? Would it be more helpful to encourage a more appropriate person to share at a more appropriate time?

Not only do we need an understanding of why we are sharing, but also we need to discriminate *with whom* we share confidences. If you picture your family in that multigenerational home, know that you do not need to stand naked in front of your whole family. There is room for privacy. Curtains can be drawn around you, or you and certain others. By choosing safe people to share your confidential information with, you have developed an intact, flexible boundary. You choose when the curtain is drawn or closed, or whether or not the window blinds are pulled up or partially opened.

The curtain of confidentiality replaces the rigid, cement-walled boundary of secrecy that blocked out all opportunity to create healthy relationships. In recovery you learn to develop boundaries, and to trust your internal cues to know with whom and when to share.

When the whole truth is told about the past, because it has been previously discounted, possibly even feared, it can be a real shock to the family system as a whole and to the internal systems of the family members. As we begin to talk openly about what has happened around those experiences in the past, we may choose to do so gradually.

Take time to think of what secrets you are maintaining and how they may be hurtful to you. With each secret identify any fear(s) you have about disclosure.

Who would you like to have this information?

What has gotten in the way of your telling them?

Who might be someone you feel safe sharing this information with?

Telling a secret for the first time is a very powerful experience. We may feel great relief and exhilaration. The telling may tap a deep well of grief and pain. It is healthier for you to first share this information with someone you trust and you know will be able to listen to what you have to say. This person is often not one who is affected personally by the information. It may feel safer to share this information with a friend, a partner or spouse, another member of a support or self-help group, a counselor, therapist, or physician. Begin where it is safest.

We benefit by hearing our words expressed out loud, allowing others the opportunity to offer us support and/or validation, either for our experiences and feelings, or for what we need to do. The sharing of confidences lessens shame, relieves burdens, and in many cases, heightens intimacy.

A turning point will come when you can identify a safe way to share the secret.

FAMILY STORIES

When we address family secrets, we are also creating new family stories. But first, it is helpful to identify old stories. As you read previously, one of Merle's family stories was that you don't share potentially painful information with the affected person; instead, you try to safeguard their options and make decisions for them. With a commitment to recovery, Merle's intent is for the family story to be rewritten so her family today supports each other as they may be faced with difficult choices.

How would you like to rewrite your story? Consider again that metaphor comparing your family to a large home with many rooms. There is a new room that is yours for the making. You can decorate it any way you want; you can fill it with the best of your things. You have choices about whom you invite to come in. You can make decisions about how you act in your own room and in the other rooms that make up your extended family's home. Your own room, your own rules—a somewhat frightening, yet clearly exciting opportunity!

IDENTIFYING FAMILY ROLES

Another significant change in the old homestead comes with the change of family roles. When you change how you interact with others in your family, you are, in effect, changing your role.

In the early years of understanding children from alcoholic families, it was extremely helpful for people to identify their own role in the context of their family. The concept of family roles became important because it offered a framework that helped affected families understand what was happening in their lives. This also made possible a language for them to talk about their experiences.

In addition, the newly discovered understanding of family roles offered validation to those who had an ability to "look good" to outsiders, but on the inside experienced great pain. The roles and the resulting restrictions helped Adult Children understand why it took so long for their pain to begin to show. Also, this was the first time the addicted family began to be addressed as a system. The labeling of roles has also been extremely helpful in addressing the problems of dysfunctional families whose issue was something other than addiction.

By identifying our own role in the context of our families, we are able to recognize many of our strengths and vulnerabilities.

The awareness of your own role is a turning point.

Roles We Have Played

As we address the ways we have been affected by families, and begin to change the ways we relate to others as well as ourselves, we will find ourselves moving from a position of one rigid role (or a combination of roles) to building from the strengths of each of them. Today, there are several versions of family roles, most emanating from the original work of renowned family therapist Virginia Satir. However, as we look at how we change in our relationships, I will address the roles as I wrote about them in *It Will Never Happen To Me*—the Responsible Child, the Adjuster, the Placater, and the Acting Out Child.

Virtually everyone has strong survival instincts. As children, many of us needed those instincts to stay alive. When our environment was not a safe place, when it didn't have the structure, the order, or the predictability we needed, we did whatever was necessary to create it. That experience became the basis for our survival roles.

Each role offers intrinsic rewards to the individual person and to the family. Responsible children, for example, bring order to the family chaos, facilitating for themselves and their siblings a predictable environment. In doing so, they personally feel a sense of greater control, and often they experience external rewards. Adjusters play a more passive role, contributing to the family stability by being invisible, not having any expectations or demands, creating an emotional insulator around themselves.

The Placaters take care of other family members' emotional needs, attempting to alleviate the pain so they feel greater stability and then are also less aware of their own pain. Placaters are often liked for being so caring. The Acting Out children are attempting to be the voice for the family, saying "HELP!" or "Look at us!"

Looking back, most adults see that they played not just one role, but a combination of roles. The majority of people, nonetheless, identify with one predominant role, and that they operated within the other roles on certain occasions. As an example, a person may identify most strongly with having been an Acting Out child, and to a lesser degree an Adjuster. Or one may have been both a Placater and the Responsible child.

For the person exploring his or her own roles, and the associated assets and liabilities, it is most helpful to look at each identified role separately from any others. It is easier to identify the strengths and deficits of each individual role, rather than two or more roles in any combination.

As people move into adulthood, they take with them the identity of their family role(s). A person who had been the Responsible Child will most often continue to demonstrate that in adult relationships, by being a leader and being goal-oriented. Susan, who was the Responsible Child in her family, maintained that position. She worked her way through law school, graduating with honors. By age thirty-one, she was in private practice as an attorney. But, she was in private practice because she couldn't work as a team member. She needed to be in charge at all times. She had difficulty listening, and she was fearful of others who made decisions. By this time, her third marriage was in trouble; she had no women friends.

People who identify with being the Adjuster still tend to need someone else to provide structure for them to react to. Steve was a man of many hopes and dreams, but too frightened to make new decisions. He could adapt to any predicament, and found his talent in working in corporations that when they said jump, he did! Move—he did! Fire so and so, he did. He had three managers in three years. While other peers were upset, he thrived on change and unpredictability. Initially, his wife of three years liked that he seemed able to listen and that he was so "flexible," but now she demanded some things from him that were very scary. She wanted him so show conviction and initiative, to express his own thoughts. He was too malleable!

The Placater, in adult life, continues to take care of people's emotional needs. Emily, at age thirty-two, was still the "family referee." She had passed up two job promotions because, if she left the area, she thought, "Who would protect Mom?"

While the strengths of these roles are so clear during the growing-up years, it is in adulthood that the deficits of theses roles truly begin to show. The Acting Out children are the ones most apt to have experienced some form of direct intervention. These people are often in trouble with society in their young adulthood, and so become parts of systems, such as hospitals or jails. And either they stay a part of such systems or their role changes, most often as a result of the intervention.

Because many people use alcohol and drugs in their acting out, a great many of them move into adulthood with an even greater likelihood of becoming addicted. At age forty-six, Patty was still acting out her anger. In spite of having a college degree, her addiction got in the way of working in her field. She supported herself by bartending instead. Known for her belligerent attitude, she challenged nearly anyone who was in an authority position, from the local policemen to her bosses. As a result, few people welcomed her presence and Patty knew it. While Patty remains angry and addicted, many of these people are sober and recovering today.

Not all Acting Out people become addicted. Depending on the depth of their anger and challenge of roles and authority, some, in fact, have mainstreamed into society better than others, having managed to redirect the strength of their skills.

Re-Evaluating Our Roles

As much as we strive to create a healthier balance in our lives, we still struggle with what we want to keep and what we want to give up in terms of survivorship. After all, we never know when we may need to call upon those survival skills again! As you work on recovering your real self, you have the chance to see yourself in the roles you have played, and to identify the strengths and deficits that have been part of each one. Once you have done this, it becomes easier to recognize what deficits of those roles you need to let go and what strengths you want to develop.

Listed below are the strengths and deficits that most often accompany each of the family roles:

Responsible Child

Strengths	*Deficits*	
Organized	Inability to listen	Inability to follow
Leadership skills	Inability to play	Inability to relax
Decision-maker	Lack of spontaneity	Severe need to be
Initiator	Inflexibility	in control
Perfectionist	High fear of mistakes	Need to be right
Goal-oriented	Inability to ask for input	
Self-disciplined		

Adjuster

Strengths	*Deficits*
Flexibility	Inability to initiate
Ability to follow	Fearful of making decisions
Easy-going attitude	Lack of direction
Not upset by negative	Inability to perceive options, power
situations	Follows without questioning

Placater

Strengths	*Deficits*
Caring	Inability to receive
Empathetic	Inability to focus on self
Good listener	Guilty
Sensitive to others	High tolerance for inappropriate behavior
Gives well	Strong fear of anger
Nice smile	
Warm	

Acting Out Child

Strengths	*Deficits*
Close to own feelings	Inappropriate expression of anger
Ability to lead (They just lead in the wrong direction)	Inability to follow direction
Less denial, greater honesty	Social problems at young ages, i.e., truancy, addiction, teen pregnancy, high school drop-out, etc..
Creative	
Sense of Humor	Intrusive

Beliefs Give Strength To Our Roles

It is easy to see that many of the strengths are just that—strengths that are valued. The problem is that they may have been learned in a context of fear, and so we still operate with fear as a cloud to those behaviors. Or, they were learned in a vacuum; therefore, we didn't learn the value of the opposite perspective. We may have learned to lead, but not follow, for instance. Or, we practiced a strength to the extreme, such as being flexible to the point that we couldn't make a commitment to any one position.

Individuals' experiences within their families are different due to many variables, i.e., birth order, ethnic origin, cultural values, economic circumstances, etc. These variables come into play when they are the source of our core beliefs. The beliefs we are taught, and those beliefs we pick up on our own, become the reasons our individual strengths become stronger and, eventually, a rigidly repeated pattern of behavior, i.e., an identifiable role. The behaviors are often fueled by our beliefs.

The following are some examples of beliefs we hold that drive our behavior:

Beliefs of the Responsible Child:

"If I don't do it, no one will."

"If I don't do this, something bad will happen, or things will get worse."

Beliefs of the Adjuster Child:

"If I don't get emotionally involved, I won't get hurt."

"I can't make a difference anyway."

"It is best to not draw attention to myself."

Beliefs of the Placater Child:

"If I am nice, people will like me."

"If I focus on someone else, the focus won't be on me and that is good."

"If I take care of you, you won't leave me or reject me."

Beliefs of the Acting Out Child:

"If I scream loudly enough, someone may notice me."

"Take what you want. No one is going to give you anything."

When you are in a painful family system, each of these positions provides some kind of reward. So, for example, the Responsible One finds that life is more predictable, stable. There are often societal rewards for good grades in school, a strong job performance, a pat on the head by parents and community members, etc... For these behaviors, then, the Adjuster is less apt to be singled out for negative attention. The Placater is apt to be complimented and to draw positive attention. The Acting Out Child is rewarded with attention. (And even when negative behavior invites negative attention, that is often experienced as better than no attention.)

Feelings Associated With Our Roles

The family role we have adopted, along with the associated beliefs, affects not only our behavior, but also what we do about our feelings. Of course, we all have feelings, but our response is very often in accordance with the beliefs, strengths, and deficits of our role.

Here are some examples of responses to feelings as affected by our roles:

The Responsible Child: "I must stay in control of my feelings."
The Adjuster: "Why should I feel? It's better if I don't."
The Placater: "I must take care of others' feelings."
The Acting Out Child: "I am angry about it, whatever it is."

Another way roles restrict our lives is that they dictate the way shame may manifest itself:

The Responsible Child shows shame with control, perfectionism, compulsivity.

The Adjuster shows shame with procrastination, victimization.

The Placater shows shame with victimization, depression, perfection.

The Acting Out Child shows shame with rage and addictions, procrastination.

While the statements above are subjective generalizations, they describe the reality that many people live.

WHO AM I, IF I'M NOT WHO I'VE BEEN?

Transformation Of Roles From Childhood To Adult Life

Our family roles have come to frame our role and related behaviors in all aspects of life—in our choices about careers, partners, friends, family, children, co-workers, and the way we feel about ourselves.

These roles have framed our sense of identity. In recovery we ask, "Who am I, if I am not the role I have played all my life?"

"Who am I, if I am not the Placater?"
"Who am I, if I am not the Acting Out Child?"
"Who am I, if I am not the Responsible Child?"

You are who you always have been—your same inner self, creative, curious, hungry, wanting, good, a valuable being. Often expressions from that inner person were ignored, punished, or never developed. You no longer need your role as your survival shield, because you no longer need to take a protective stance against shame or fear.

When our worth and our identity is no longer defined by a survival role, we have choices about meeting our own needs and developing in our own ways that we didn't have before. We don't necessarily develop a new personality, but we experience life without the need to defend against pain, and that means we are different in how we interact in the world. But is it all that good to be different, you may wonder? Certainly; at the same time we let go of the shield, we honor that role because it served a wonderful purpose, by helping us survive. Then the question arises, "What about the strengths you have had?"

Here are some of the kinds of specific questions people have:

"I am a nurse professionally. If I recover from caretaking everybody, does that mean I will have to change careers?"

"Anger is the only feeling I have ever known. Do I have to give it up?"

"My being so responsible and organized has made me a lot of money. I am a very successful businessman. Will recovery take that away?"

"Flexibility is my name. Will I lose that quality if I look at these issues?"

Recovery does not mean that you are saying goodbye to the

strengths of the role! While you want to keep the strengths, you can learn skills that create greater balance in your life. You can develop skills to replace the deficits of the role, and you can learn the skills of the other roles. Part of your new development comes with understanding why you act and react as you do. Another part is practice, revising your beliefs as you explore and question them, and gradually risking new behaviors that are congruent with what you really think and feel.

As you attend to the issues that cause you pain or restrict your personal freedom, you begin to develop a more rounded sense of self. You will not need the role to be the source of your worth, your identity. You will be defining your self from a broader perspective— a perspective of ascertaining your own values. You will be able to listen to your internal cues about what you need. You will have created belief systems that support a way of life you choose, versus a protective stance against shame or fear. And, at the same time, you can honor that the shield of your role helped you survive and so served a wonderful purpose.

These are the gifts you can maintain or develop:

The Responsible Adult—

Maintains leadership skills, ability to organize, initiative, but lets go of the need to be in control;

Develops the ability to listen, to follow, flexibility, ability to relax.

The Adjuster—

Maintains flexibility, ability to be a team player;

Develops ability to initiate, make decisions, perceive options.

The Placater—

Maintains their empathy and diplomatic skills;

Develops ability to care for self, ability to prioritize for self.

The Acting Out Adult—
Maintains ability to identify own anger, to speak truth, ability to lead;
Develops ability to lead in more positive direction, healthy expression of anger, problem-solving skills.

As we re-examine the roles that have defined our lives, recovering the strengths, letting go of the deficits, and developing skills we need, we also have to examine and revise our old beliefs, as I have pointed out, for these are the beliefs that supported and actually gave impetus to our behaviors. Earlier in this chapter we looked at the beliefs associated with each role. Now let's look at the ways these beliefs can be transformed.

Responsible Adult beliefs transform—
From: "If I don't do it, no one will."
       "If I don't do this, something bad will happen or things will get worse."
       "I am not of value unless I am being productive."
To: "If I don't do it, someone else will and that is okay."
       "If I don't do it, it will be done differently, and that is okay."
       "I am of value 'being,' not just doing."

Obviously, we have to get to a place of acceptance where it is really okay for someone else to do those things we normally would. We have to come to believe we are worthy and of value even when we are not doing all the performing, even when we are not being productive. It is okay to just 'be.'

Adjuster beliefs transform—
From: "If I do not get emotionally involved, I won't get hurt."
       "I can't make a difference."
       "It is best to not draw attention to myself."
To: "If I don't get emotionally involved, I will never have a meaningful connection."

"I do make a difference. I am of value and people will value me."

"I deserve attention."

While we seldom seek the 'star' role, we come to feel comfortable in our visibility. We can feel a strength we did not allow ourselves to appreciate previously.

Placater beliefs transform —

From: "If I am nice, people will like me."

"If I focus on someone else, the focus won't be on me."

"If I take care of you, you won't leave me or reject me."

To: "I am likeable without having to take care of others."

"It is okay to have the focus. I am deserving."

"I don't have the power to keep you with me, and if you stay, it is   because of who I am, not what I do for you."

We learn to take care of ourselves as well as we have others. We recognize that selfishness is not bad, it is an act of self-care.

Acting Out beliefs transform—

From: "If I put my face in theirs, they will notice me."

"Take what you want—no one is going to give you anything."

"My needs override everyone else's."

To: "I can ask for what I want and listen to the other person at the same time."

"While my needs are important, others' needs are to be acknowledged as well."

"The world is not out to get me. I'm not here alone."

Redirecting all of that energy put into trying to get your needs met by challenging the world will allow an increase in self-esteem and a connection to others that will create an ongoing, natural high.

Rethinking our beliefs and re-evaluating our behaviors sets us up to relate to our families, partners, children, and friends in a much healthier manner in every aspect of our lives.

ENDING OLD ROLES

Just as recovery is a process, not an event, so is the task of identifying and re-evaluating the roles we have played. These roles are as old as our attempts to protect ourselves from pain. The resulting behaviors have become a matter of habit, and the beliefs that have fueled them spring up almost automatically. Paradoxically, the roles do not bring us safety or freedom from pain. They restrict our lives in ways we can scarcely recognize, and they are the present-day cause of much needless pain. Clearly, as Betty Ford said in her book on recovery, to free ourselves from these old ways is "a glad awakening."

The task of recovering our unique selves, as we revise and renew our current ways of being, begins with awareness.

The awareness that we have adopted a protective role is a turning point.

The awareness that we no longer need that role to survive is a turning point.

6
Recovery Is The Road
To Yourself

New Ways of Being, New Ways of Relating

"Each man's life represents a road toward himself."
—Hermann Hesse

"Recovery is accepting yourself for who you are—no longer waiting for others
to define you or approve of you."
—Claudia Black, *It's Never Too Late To Have A Happy
Childhood*

Recovery is the road toward your unique self. Many of the Hasidic
"legendary anecdotes" emphasize the uniqueness of every person.

"When I get to heaven," said Rabbi Zusya, " they will not ask
me: 'Why were you not more like Moses?' Instead they will ask,
'Why were you not more like yourself?' "

Recovery is about discovering and becoming your own, true self,
the essence that is you behind the masks you have put on and the
personas you have played while you were trying to please the world
around you and keep would-be predators away. What you did—adopt-
ing rules and roles to keep yourself a safe distance from others—
also created a distance within yourself, a gap between the real you
and that unreal, defensive other.

However, today you have the opportunity to live with choice,
rather than to continue a script. Up until now, how you have con-

nected with others has been based on maintaining childhood beliefs and behaviors. No longer operating from a basis of fear and shame, you can more easily let go of childhood family rules and roles. When you do, you will find a freedom in relationships not previously experienced.

Relationships, be they with friends, family, or co-workers, have the potential for interdependence rather than dependency or rigid autonomy. You no longer have to go through life in one up/one down relationships. With just your changes, relationships have a greater chance to experience mutual support because you are engaging from a position of self-responsibility. When you interact with others who are not operating from a position of health, you are still acting from a position of positive self-regard and self-care. You are being true to you.

BEGINNING NEW RELATIONSHIPS

Yet, as promising as new and renewed relationships can be, leaving the past ways of connecting behind means leaving familiar territory and entering the unknown. Once, when your father raged and you placated him, you could predict that the storm would blow over and calm would return. Or, when you took responsibility for making everyone happy, working until you were exhausted or ill, you could assume that your family would come home that evening so at least you weren't left alone. If you make changes and rock the boat, so to speak, what will happen then?

Uncertainty is one of the things people will face when they make changes. Another is that many people tend to continue in old family roles for fear they will lose face in front of each other. How can the once Responsible Child look to the Adjuster for support? And then how will that Adjuster respond? Will the family trust the Acting Out child to take on adult responsibilities now? Will the family reinforce the Placater's guilt or become angry when the Placater doesn't remove family pain? These unknowns can be very frightening to you as you begin your recovery.

When you begin to heal, it is very typical to be enthusiastic about sharing this healing process with others in your family. Yet, very often they are inwardly upset or still in denial, and so they react with a blank look, or an even more emphatic verbal response: "What are you talking about?" "I don't know whose parents you are talking about, but they aren't mine!" or "How could you be raised in an alcoholic family when I wasn't?" To have significant others blatantly ignore, discount, or deny your reality can be very startling. And, even when there is the support of some family members, it can be very surprising how different your experience is compared to your brothers or sisters.

What we need to recognize is that while we are in a healing process, our family members may have not yet chosen the same path. Our idealistic thinking gets in the way of being able to understand that.

Relationships And Expectations

The key for anyone who wants a healthy relationship has to do with expectations. Having relationships with individuals who are not in the growing process has to be limiting. They cannot be as honest, open, nor as nurturing. They may be intrusive and inappropriate in their behavior and expectations. It is crucial, then, for you to adjust your expectations and to recognize and accept the limitations.

When you try to get your needs met by someone who is incapable or unwilling, disappointment is sure to follow. When you stop expecting to get what can't or won't be given, the relationship becomes healthier for you.

If the other person in the relationship is very important in your life, a parent or a partner, for example, you certainly have the right to tell them what you need, but even though they may be very close to you, they still may not be capable or willing—and that is what you need to be able to hear.

The turning point in your relationship is the awareness that your growth is not about getting other people to change.

Your loved ones are not necessarily asking or choosing to live their lives differently. It is true that when change occurs, it creates the potential for change among others. The changes they see in us may be the kinds of things they desire for themselves. You may be a model that offers them hope. But, the bottom line is, this recovery process is about you and you creating change for yourself. Everything else that comes is an unexpected gift.

Difficult Family Relationships: Staying Connected With Limitations

The struggle for so many recovering adults is how to interact with members of their childhood family, their parents and siblings. Cultural and family values influence the messages and feelings you received regarding family loyalty and commitment. Typically, we want to stay connected with our families. But, how do you re-enter the arena of family relationships and be true to who you are and what you believe? Your efforts may be tentative at first; you will have to learn somewhat from trial and error. Everyone's situation is unique and every individual will need to sort through these issues in a way that is comfortable to them.

It is common to hear adults in recovery express loneliness and sadness that their recovery has further alienated them from various members of the family. When a family has not developed healthy alliances, communication patterns, etc., one family member's recovery is often confusing for the non-recovering members.

So often, being with family members means having more superficial interactions, sharing the daily routine without intimacy, recreational interactions, carrying on family rituals, i.e., baptisms, holiday dinners, bar mitzvahs. These traditional occasions can be one way to maintain connection to ones you love. Even superficial contact provides connection. It may be that your choice (and, remember, you *do* have choices here) is to choose this level of involvement over no involvement at all.

It is helpful to know why we are visiting with family. Do we feel a sense of loyalty, or duty, enjoyment, or love? Again, people differ as to their history and values, which impacts decisions about being loyal and dutiful. In spite of family pain, many people still feel love, and many people have found ways to enjoy certain family members. Or, are we still unconsciously seeking validation or approval? It doesn't seem to matter how old we are, we all want to know that we are valued by our parents. When we didn't receive that validation in our growing-up years, it often becomes an even more urgent, yet usually denied, need. Unfortunately, validation and approval are not as apt to be offered by sick or unhealthy parents. They are often no more capable of offering that to us today than they were when we were children. In fact, very likely they are seeking that very same validation from us now.

People differ in their ways of connecting. In Amy's family, she is the only one in recovery. Still, Amy and her codependent mother are able to take weekend holidays now and then. They enjoy sightseeing together, and when visiting in each other's homes, they connect through local gossip and conversations about favorite television programs. For a while, Amy took walks through the woods with her alcoholic father. Today, her father is senile, drinking little now due to frailty and age, but the two of them talk about the leaves, the squirrels, the trees, and weather.

Amy's visits with her two sisters are less frequent because their differences are too blatant; there is too much potential for conflict, so their conversations are limited to the tasks of their daily routines. Certainly, Amy would like more intimacy and more authentic sharing, but without greater changes on the part of family, it won't occur.

Nearly all relationships will have certain limitations. By recognizing these limitations, we can be realistic in our expectations and far less disappointed by others' attitudes and behaviors. So, in Amy's case, she recognizes and grieves her loss, accepts the reality, and makes her choices. Then she develops other relationships in her life that are more intimate and, in many cases, will provide her with another, healthier "family bond."

It is common to hear people in recovery refer to others as their "family of choice." Maternal or paternal needs are met by older, mentor friends. Sister- and brother-like relationships are developed with peers close to their age. Some adults actually develop a friendship with a person close to their child's age, so they can give to that younger person in ways they had not able to give to their own child at that age. This relationship option is not intended to negate the parent's earlier experience, but by acknowledging the parent-child loss, there is an opportunity for healing, intimacy, and growth.

While you lived in the same house, survived a difficult history together, there may be no emotional sense of connection at all. This usually occurs with siblings more than parents, but certainly may be true for both. When a lack of emotional bonding is mutual, family members seldom even attempt to connect. Unfortunately, when it is not a mutual feeling, one person is often left feeling rejection and confusion. The other person, without the sense of connection, is often feeling burdened, harassed and confused, expecting and wanting less in a relationship. It is healthier if you can take responsibility and graciously let the person know you aren't going to make that transition to becoming more connected. This will be a loss for you and one you will grieve, but can transcend.

Maintaining Your Recovery As You Relate To Your Family

The challenge in relationships with people who aren't in recovery is to maintain the integrity of your healing as you do so. To take care of yourself, it is essential to re-define limits and boundaries. When family members are still in the throes of denial, delusion, frozen feelings, addictions, or compulsions, how much time can you spend with them before the relationship begins to deteriorate? How long before you lose sense of your integrity—in other words, how long before you feel unable to maintain your own boundaries? It may be twenty minutes, or it could be two hours, or three days.

To take care of yourself in relationships that are difficult for you, reflect back to what has been the pattern in the past and then plan accordingly. If communication seems to deteriorate after fifteen minutes, limit visits to ten minutes. Setting time limits applies to telephone calls as well. You may find the first few minutes are okay, but after that, the old ways go into effect.

In terms of longer visits, you may need to limit the amount of time you spend with parents: rather than spend one week, stay three days; rather than spend all day, stay three hours. Again, the question is, "What period of time can you be with your parents before you revert to old behaviors?"

Determine for yourself at what points in your family contacts you find yourself not responding as you would like. Use these cues for your limits. Remember, you don't have to decide between "all or nothing," i.e., between giving them all you assume they want and never seeing them again. There are almost any number of choices in between these extremes.

Another point to remember is that, while we need to own our past role, we do not need to give up the strengths that were part of it. In Barbara's family she was the Responsible Child. Now she says, "I was the responsible child growing up, and I continue that in my relationship with my parents." What we give up and what we don't are entirely ours to choose. The important concern is that we no longer make decisions from fear of rejection or need for approval. It is crucial to see that, truly, we have a choice.

As you take care of yourself in ongoing relationships with family or friends who tend to operate from the old, hurtful patterns of behavior, you may need to establish boundaries around your conversations. Certain subjects may be taboo because they only lead to old behaviors, i.e., "I will not engage in discussion with mother about my oldest sister because nothing positive comes from it." Is having a subject be taboo the same as having a Don't Talk Rule? No. You would be willing to discuss the subject if it could be discussed openly, honestly.

The most important guideline for relationships is to decide what you are willing to do and not do:

— What you are willing to talk about and not talk about? Are there certain conversations you are willing to engage in and others not? Do you need to tell your family ahead of time?

— Are there certain times of the day that are better than others for telephone calls or visiting? For example, if your mother is drinking by noon, visit her in the morning. (By the way, do let her know why she doesn't see you in the afternoons.)

Another necessary point of business is to plan what you need for emotional support prior to your family contact. Let's say you are visiting parents for three days. You may find it helpful, or even necessary, to take daily walks by yourself, to go to a Twelve Step meeting, call your sponsor, take your own healthy food, continue exercise, and/or read meditation books.

Unfortunately, for some people family interactions only result in pain. As a result, some Adult Children choose to remove themselves— at least physically—from any and all relationship with their parent(s) and/or other family members, believing they will feel and be better with the distance between family member(s) and them. While this may be a healthy decision for some, the all-or-nothing aspect of it is usually not healthy for most.

This is a choice you have and it is your relationship and family history that must be the deciding factors. If you do separate yourself physically from your family, be aware that you will still need to take responsibility for your "script" from that family system. Until grieved and healed, you will still be left with your fears, anger, guilts, dysfunctional belief systems, and old defense mechanisms. All too often we take our issues of shame, fear, and powerlessness with us into the other areas of our lives.   Remember, the choice to maintain a family relationship is now yours.

Sibling Connections

Siblings within the same family experience life very differently. When Susan was seven, the family took vacations together, visited amusement parks on weekends, and laughed at her father's antics at the dinner table. By the time her younger sister Dana was the same age, their parents had divorced. Vacations and weekend excursions were too expensive for her mother; dinners were often eaten alone with her sister while their mother was still at work.

There are many variables that affect the development of different personalities in children. Not only are children very different personalities from birth, but also, each child enters the family at a different stage in the family's life. One of the major considerations is that each child enters the family at a different place in the progression of the dysfunctions that plague many families.

A clear example of this is when one parent passes from social drinking to problem drinking to becoming an alcoholic. Those children who had access to either the alcoholic or co-alcoholic parent in the earlier stages or pre-stages have the opportunity of receiving healthier parenting. They may receive more consistency and predictability, which leads to a greater sense of security. They may receive a more consistent show of love, which helps build the child's ability to trust. Typically, the middle and younger children miss the opportunity to experience a healthy (even if sometimes short-lived) family environment. For them, family life is more disruptive and chaotic in their formative years. As a result of birth position in the family, each child has different perceptions and has learned a different style of survival.

Whether a family's life is chaotic as a result of some member's addiction, or a family is rigid and emotionally isolating, the result is a lack of bonding between siblings. Yet, it is typical that you, as one who is in the process of healing past pain, will want to try to put the pieces of your history together, and in so doing, explore the issue of distance between you and siblings.

Siblings are the witnesses to each other's shame. In each other's presence we mirror back the hurt, disappointment, fear, anger, and shame of our early years. No wonder our contacts are superficial—that helps avoid remembering our pain. We develop telephone relationships rather than one-to-one contact; we visit only in the company of others. Our conversations are superficial in order to avoid intimacy. We will do whatever is necessary to defend against pain.

It is possible that you grew up so emotionally isolated, and in such different stages of your family life, with different attitudes and values, that therefore you have little on which to base a relationship. I've heard several adult children say they wouldn't choose their brothers or sisters to be their friends.

Ideally, people hope to have intimate relationships within the family, but for a great many of us, that isn't our reality. Some of us have enough positive connection from childhood that, with effort, healing occurs that fosters intimacy. For others, the estrangement is too great. As a consequence, siblings may connect only through their parents, or they simply don't have contact at all.

While our pain and shame has lessened and we are ready for a more sincere relationship with siblings, they are often not yet at that place. Most likely you, the reader, are the sibling who wants a more intimate relationship. You can offer a sibling information about your experiences within the family and your healing process. As appropriate, you can explain how aspects of their life or certain behaviors are related to repressed feelings, hurtful beliefs, or lack of skill not yet learned. But you cannot control whether or not they listen, hear, and seek their own path of healing. In my experience, family members never seem to "do recovery" in our time frame, and in the order we want it.

Offer feedback as it is appropriate, and then practice the Al-Anon principle of "letting go." Stay focused on your own recovery. Remember that for many people, the business of focusing on others is a distraction from focusing on self.

Making The Transition To Your New Relationship

As you make the transition from the habits and responses from your old role to the new relationship, one crucial question is, "What becomes of your pain?" As we discussed in chapter two, there is pain from the chronic loss of the past and pain from the losses that are perpetuated by beliefs and behaviors in the present. What do you do with that pain you still feel? You must identify, confront, and resolve the source of pain so it will end, and the remaining feelings you have can be grieved and let go.

SHARING YOUR PAIN/GRIEF WITH FAMILY MEMBERS

In your recovery process, owning what occurred for you in your childhood is necessary. Sometime you, as the adult child, will need to say such things as, "I am angry that...." "It hurt when ...." "It wasn't fair that ...." etc.... This is a natural part of the grief process. It is a part of the process that allows you to own the past and put it behind you.

While these statements need to be verbalized, whether or not they are said to family members is an entirely different question. You need to have become comfortable with yourself, your feelings. You need to be "walking the walk," not just "talking the talk," before it seems appropriate to share with your family what you remember and how you feel.

You also need to have a support system. You need to have had conversations with others to become comfortable with your own truth. Then you are better able to consider what you do or do not want to share with your birth family.

The following questions are suggested as guidelines to help you explore how much of your feelings and awarenesses you want to share. As you consider talking to parents and/or siblings, think of what you would say to each of them separately. What you want to share to whom may be very different from each other.

QUESTION 1. What do you want to say?

Do you want to tell this person that you are in a healing process related to childhood pain? Do you want to describe the process of healing? Or are you wanting to share specific feelings and thoughts you have had about your life? There is a tendency to think in absolutes—"I need to tell them everything!" So, I would begin this process by thinking about what you want to say, and then welcome the thought of not having to say everything. Instead, ask "what part?" or "how much of?" In other words, ask yourself, What part of my childhood pain do I want to share? How much of what is discussed in therapy do I want to share? or Do I want to describe the rituals of a Twelve Step meeting?

QUESTION 2. Why do you want to tell him/her that?

It's important to examine your motivation for telling something. Sharing demands great honesty on your part. Will you feel better for having said it to them? Will it possibly clarify matters for you? Are you saying it to hurt them? Are you telling them things to seek their approval for what you are now doing?

Personally, I think your feelings and thoughts need to be expressed by saying them aloud. Whether or not you speak directly to the people who are the source of the pain is another question. Know your motivation. If you aren't sure, wait until you have greater clarity.

QUESTION 3. What do you hope/expect will happen?

So many times I've heard the response, "nothing," in answer to that question. That cannot be the underlying answer, because you must have some expectation or your need to talk wouldn't exist. Sometimes people aren't aware that there is a hope and an expectation until it isn't met. Many hope for an "I love you," or an "I'm sorry." Those responses are possible, but not necessarily realistic.

Our expectations are usually kept more realistic when we try to picture very specifically what another's response will be, i.e., "I expect my mother to sit as I talk to her." "I expect my father to listen."

QUESTION 4. How realistic is that hope/expectation?

Whenever parents are told that their parenting has been anything less than positive, parents will feel guilt and pain. They may feel sad, angry, embarrassed, ashamed. They may cry or become angry. To expect them not to feel hurt is unrealistic. The intensity to which they experience that pain is related to the circumstances in which and how you present the information as well as their own emotional and mental health. This does not mean that you should not share. It is simply a fact that you need to be prepared for.

Keep your expectations and hopes low. Most adults have never experienced their family having a recovery process. Unrecovered family members most likely will maintain their position of guilt, hurt, or anger. If there is little or no recovery on their part, they will often repeat their old patterns of ignoring you, screaming, blaming, crying, or giving you a token acknowledgement.

A family member whose life has been changed by their own recovery process may be able to hear you today. Yet, be realistic. They will feel hurt. At the same time it may be of greater value for you to share with them and allow them to feel their own pain than for you not to share with them.

Many Adult Children have shared with both recovering and nonrecovering family, and have felt relief and validation for the experience. Many have also received the long sought "I love you," or "I'm sorry." The more you pre-think the situation, are clear about what you want to say, consider the timing, clarify your expectations to be realistic, the more positive the outcome.

I would suggest taking the above four questions and writing out your responses to them. Often times when we write we are more honest than when we keep our thoughts in our head.

Sharing about recovery or the thoughts and feelings you have during the healing process is an intimate disclosure. Do give thought to the timing, the place in which you begin to share. I am not suggesting a tightly controlled setting, but sometimes we set ourselves up for what feels like rejection because we choose the wrong setting. While everybody's situations differ, typically weddings, funerals, bar mitzvahs, birthdays, and holidays are not the most appropriate times. Unfortunately, because you may seldom spend time with family outside of such an occasion, that may limit opportunities. Simply, give thought to when you choose to share such intimacies.

A Word Of Caution About Sharing

People in recovery can become very verbal with even strangers about their histories, their feelings. They also listen to others pour their hearts out. As a result, when they share with family they often do so with the zeal experienced in their twelve step or therapy group, expecting equally reciprocal self-disclosure. Be realistic in your expectations. You may have more experience trusting the process of honesty than they do.

I suggest that you never share such newly discovered intimate thoughts with family without having shared them first with your therapist, a sponsor, other group members, whoever is a part of your recovery process. There is so much power in saying things for the very first time—we need to hear ourselves.

Beth, who has been in therapy for six months, is travelling, and has an opportunity to visit her practicing alcoholic father, asks, "I'm seeing my father and I want to tell him about me." When asked what that means, she exclaims, "I want to tell him how angry I am!" Know that Beth has not seen her father in seven years. Their adult visits have been superficial at best, and a Christmas card from Beth to her Dad in recent years has been her only form of communication. For Beth to share the depth and intensity of her anger after six months of therapy most likely will not be productive. Beth is discovering her anger for the first time in thirty-three years. She is speaking the words for the first time. She needs to know more about herself, her anger, to develop a line of communication with Dad, to think in terms of "what part of her anger, how much of her anger," sort out expectations, and have a support system more ingrained in her life.

We also feel a sense of urgency that is not always warranted. Joe, twenty-two, who has been in therapy for seven weeks, says "I need to fly home and see my mom and tell her about all my new thoughts and my feelings about our family." Knowing Joe was planning to see his mother in three months at Christmas, I questioned the urgent need to fly home sooner. Joe responded with, "Well, she could be dead by Christmas." Assuming I missed an important fact regarding his mother being either (1) terminally ill or (2) very old, I inquired, wherein he told me, "She is old. She is forty-six and what if something happens to her by Christmas?" Clearly Joe was reacting to the fear that, should his mother die before he was able to see her, he would forever have unfinished business with her. Yet, realistically, Joe's mother is not high risk to an imminent death, and he was so new to his recovery, he would benefit by more time in therapy before he shared so intimately with his mother.

CONFRONTATION AS A PART OF SHARING, AS A WAY TO ENDING THE SOURCE OF THE PAIN

Sharing and confronting are all a part of the same continuum. But when people think of confronting someone, they are usually thinking of sharing what that person did that was hurtful. Implicit in this question is, how important is it to one's personal mental health to present specific information about the pain you have experienced to the person who is most directly responsible?

There are many advantages to confrontation. Here are some of the most important ones:

1. Confronting is a way to resolve or bring closure to the relationship or part of the relationship that plagues you. Bringing closure is important because unresolved relationships will continue to bother you until you get things out in the open and deal with them. The internal conflict over how and if you should confront can cause you to have continual imaginary conversations with the person(s), obsessing about how they would react, what they might say. Obsessing resolves nothing.

2. Confronting provides an opportunity to set the record straight, or to communicate what you need from that person now. Confronting those who have hurt you not only gives them another chance but presents you with another chance to resolve an important issue.

3. If you don't have a confrontation with those who have hurt you, you will tend to have inappropriate confrontations with others instead.

4. Confronting those who have hurt you enables you to take back

your power, proving to yourself that you are no longer going to allow anyone to frighten or control you.

5. Confronting those who have caused you damage and pain can help to assure that you will not continue to be victimized. When you confront you break the cycle of victimization.

6. Confronting is a way of breaking through the denial.

Advantages And Disadvantages For Confronting

Now, whether you confront face-to-face is another question. Speaking the truth out loud is vital, but whether or not it is said to the person directly is another question. This is usually the more difficult dilemma for people. Again, not knowing your circumstances, it is difficult for any writer to advise, but the following advantages and disadvantages to face-to-face and then symbolic forms of confrontation may be helpful to you.

The advantages of sharing face to face are:
1. You see the person's reactions to what you are saying. This helps you to discover how the person really feels about what you are saying, about what occurred, about you.
2. It is harder for the other person to ignore what you are saying.
3. It offers opportunity to talk it out at length.

Disadvantages to a face-to-face discussion are:
1. The person you are confronting may resort to the very behaviors that were once hurtful to you, i.e. verbal abuse, physical abuse, condemnation, mockery, prayer vigil, etc., causing you to feel confused or frightened.
2. You may not want to know the other person's response. You may just want to say your piece without hearing a reaction.
3. The other person's response may confuse you or distract you, and you may end up saying things you really don't mean.

4. You may find the other person is too busy thinking up a defense to actually hear what you have to say.

You are not a coward if you choose not to confront face-to-face.

Less risky, yet still direct forms of confrontation are using the telephone or sending a letter. These have some of the advantages stated, but without the risks.

Indirect/symbolic ways of confronting are through the use of therapy techniques such as gestalt, role play, psychodrama, letter writing (letters that are not sent, given to, or read to the person).

Advantages to these indirect/symbolic methods are:
1. You are free to say what you need to without fearing their reaction.
2. You can maintain the safety of distance and still gain closure in the relationship.

Disadvantages to these methods are:
1. You may feel as if you missed out on having the chance to confront directly.
2. You may wonder what it would have felt like to speak your mind. If you do not choose to confront directly, however, it does not exclude the possibility of doing the direct confronting at another time.

If you choose a more direct method, do some problem-solving in advance, planning the place, the setting, and what you will say. Practice what you will say. Know what is most important and plan to say that first.

Again, be realistic about the kinds of responses you might get. If someone has abused you in the past, it is unlikely that person will suddenly become sensitive to your needs. Disclosure of abuse usually disrupts a family system of denial. Often, family members find the exposure so threatening that they turn the survivor into a scapegoat, denying her experiences, minimizing or blaming her. Various other family members call to berate you, tell you that you are wrong, or even bad, for saying what you are saying. They attempt to punish you by not being willing to talk to you, or they will no longer acknowledge you or your children. In extreme cases, some adult children have been taken out of wills. When other members of your family also have been abused, and have either repressed it entirely or want to avoid feeling the pain around it, unearthing these feelings can be so threatening, or can imply such changes, the family will reject the survivor altogether rather than deal with her.

Therefore, it is essential that you approach any confrontation by focusing on what you need to say rather than on any response you may get. Stay clear for yourself, your motivation, your needs. Don't be disappointed if you plan a scenario and it turns out different than you expected. If you can stay present with your needs, your feelings, you will be okay.

HOW CAN I SHARE MY PAIN IF MY PARENT HAS DIED?

Some readers feel as if they will miss an important part of recovery because they cannot share their thoughts and feelings with a significant person who has died. When they are working on early family issues, it is most commonly a parent who has died, but it can certainly be another family member, a partner or friend with whom you would have desired sharing or confronting. These symbolic techniques provide that possibility. When someone significant dies, and hurt has been associated with your relationship to that person, there is usually much grief to be dealt with, grief of the past and for what will never be. When Rita's father died, she was confused about the intensity of her sense of loss, the physical pain that came with a very deep sadness and anger. Rita had never been close to her father. She thought she had accepted his indifference, his rejection of her. But when he died, she became profoundly aware of what she never had, nor would ever get from her father. She'd never sat and enjoyed his presence. She'd never get his approval. She'd never hear an "I love you" and she still wanted it. In addition, though, it may be the finality of their death that allows you to become mobilized in recovery. And with that you can move on in your life. That is what happened for Rita. In spite of the fact that she had been in therapy, there was another layer of grief work she would need to do in order to move on. If you have been looking at this relationship prior to the death, it is possible that much of the grief work has been completed. If so, the intensity or duration of the grief may not be so great, yet the finality of the loss pushes one to a final depth of grief and acceptance.

There are techniques, usually employed with therapists, that allow you to proceed in your process of wanting to speak to your deceased parent. Letter writing, gestalt therapy, and psychodramatic techniques can be very helpful. These techniques allow both you and your parent to speak to each other. They are symbolic forms of communication, but highly therapeutic. Some people actually visit the person's grave, to talk to the deceased. You can take a picture of the deceased, place it in a chair, and tell them what you want to say. Some people need to say, "I am angry with you for...." or "I forgive you for...." or "I want you to know these things about me...."

More than anything, you need to hear your recovery is about you—not whether or not a parent is living. It's about you and your relationship to life—and that includes coming to terms with family mortality.

PRESENT DAY RELATIONSHIPS

By letting go of past and present pain, by creating healthier beliefs and developing new skills, you will create new ways of relating, not to just the family members with whom you were raised, but others you meet in your life—friends, co-workers, partners, husbands, wives, and children. Again, you have choices about who you invite into your life and how you interact. Yet, in spite of this potential, people often flounder like fish out of water.

We had such poor modeling that we may still be confused about what creates a healthy relationship. Our expectations may be unrealistic. One of the most important concepts in creating healthy relationships is understanding that relationships have different levels and purposes. Yet, irrespective of level, there are certain characteristics that cross nearly all levels.

LEVELS OF RELATIONSHIPS

Relationships have different levels and purposes. Some people are only in our lives, and visa versa, we are only in theirs, to provide a practical service. For example, the bus driver's role is to see that we are driven safely to a destination. The barber's role is to provide a satisfactory haircut. A co-worker's role is to develop a relationship that allows the goals of the workplace to be met. The intimacy we develop with friends and partners offers a greater sense of meaning, purpose, and connectedness than do our more casual and superficial relationships. I do not want to discount that we develop caring feelings toward those who work with us or provide services, but many Adult Children overwhelm others in their life in an attempt to garner intimacy with all they meet. As a result, they often distance people in their unrealistic expectations, feel let down when others don't reciprocate, or are spread so thin they have little intimacy with anybody. They find they have less time for those they've made commitments to and more with those whose relationship is more superficial.

In our video series on relationships, Terence Gorski and I define levels of adult relationships with the predominant purpose being:

Casual Involvement	Casual involvement occurs in relationships where people interact in a casual manner and have little or no commitment to one another.
Companion	Companionship involves two persons associating for the purpose of sharing a common activity. The activity is more important than the person and the person becomes interchangeable.

Friend

Friendship is where two people associate for the purpose of mutual support and enjoyment of each other. The person is most important. The activity is secondary.

Romantic

Romantic relationships are where friendship is shared with sensuality, passion, and sexuality. Romantic love is more than passion and sexuality. Passion and sexuality can be experienced in the context of casual involvement.

Committed

Committed relationship is where we mutually agree to do what they say we are going to do. We agree to work on whatever problems arise with a mutual trust of sincerity and intent.

While it is not always reality, it is healthiest for people to move through these stages as listed. Once a relationship has moved into a romantic or committed stage, the couple continues, though, to incorporate the previous levels into their daily lives. Committed relationships incorporate casual contact from the standpoint that superficial routine is a part of daily life. For people with troubled childhoods, it is important to learn that casual contact is not abandonment. The ability to move in and out of these levels will be incorporated into a committed relationship.

As well, there can certainly be intimate moments and experiences with strangers or companions. Those who experience natural crisis at the same time, those who are witness to a beautiful scene together, may connect in a highly intimate fashion. While such moments may be fleeting in time, they may affect us for life. Those times are seldom forgotten, yet it is with our better friendships, partners, and family with whom we experience our greatest ongoing intimacy.*

CHARACTERISTICS OF A HEALTHY RELATIONSHIP

We have gone through so much of our lives making assumptions or guessing about what is normal or what is appropriate in relationships. We are many times still operating in a vacuum. As we conclude this chapter, the following list of characteristics of healthy relationships may be very helpful to you.

As you read through each characteristic, consider all your various kinds of relationships—with your parents, children, your partner, and your friends. While there are differences in degree such as, you will set different physical boundaries, how, when, and by whom you are touched; different emotional boundaries, what you share, what you are willing to listen to; and different social boundaries, where you will interact, with whom and in what capacity—each characteristic applies to each of your relationships.

1. Respect
Respect is an attitude for which courtesy is an expression. My respect is an acceptance of who you are, your autonomy, the uniqueness of you.

2. Honesty
Honesty and open communication mean that people are free to be themselves. "I have given up fear of rejection when I am less than perfect, when I am vulnerable, when it may mean you disagree with me. I can tell you my feelings, my thoughts, without fear of a major catastrophe."

Obviously, in order to be able to do this, we need to first be honest with ourselves so we can be honest with another. For some of us, this also means we may need to learn healthy communication skills, the ability to speak for oneself, and the ability to listen.

---

*A special note to certain readers: while so many people are anxious to discover intimacy in a committed relationship, I don't want you to think that if you are not in a long-term, committed relationship there is something wrong with you. Not being in such a relationship may be the healthiest position you can be in at this time. When you are not in such a relationship, you can still work on the qualities that allow intimacy with friends, self, and a higher power.

3. Realistic Expectations

We need to be realistic about what we can offer another and what they can offer us. If we have any history of growing up with en-meshed boundaries, unrealistic expectations placed on us, or even magical thinking on our part, that can cause us to be very unrealistic of ourselves and others. Be aware that the other person is not going to be available to meet all of your needs. Nor should he or she. You are responsible for many of your needs, while different people to-gether, e.g., friends, family, and partner, meet varying interpersonal needs.

Be cautious of someone trying to meet all of your needs at all times. It is likely that person is very fearful of rejection and won't be taking responsibility for themselves and hasn't developed a sense of self.

4. Trust

That means "I feel safe, psychologically and physically safe with you. I have no fears nor anxieties with respect to your treatment of me." For there to be trust, there needs to be consistency, predictabil-ity. To be trusted, a person has to demonstrate reliability, that he or she follows through with their intentions. Trust develops over time.

5. Autonomy

Intimacy is a sharing of autonomy. Real autonomy means each of us taking full responsibility for our own lives, for evolving into the best human being we can be. We are the fulfillers of our own life scripts and the exercisers of our own physical, emotional spiritual energies. With autonomy we have the ability to be clear about our own needs, being respectful to the boundaries and limits of others as well as ourselves. We are also able to honor the other person in his or her differences.

People sometimes need to be cautious, in that sometimes au-tonomy passes for unbridled, unmitigated selfishness. "To hell with the rest of the world, I am going to get what I want when I want it because I am entitled to do what I please." That is not true. No one is entitled to get what he wants when he wants it from anyone. That is selfishness, intrusiveness, and greed.

While a healthy relationship is not a power struggle between two rigidly autonomous beings, neither should it be symbiotic. The two of you do not have to think and feel the same way about all things. We want to share ourselves without collapsing into one being.

A healthy relationship is shared autonomy that grows in strength when shared.

6. Shared Power

A healthy relationship is about shared power, not control. Both people in the relationship are able to take initiative and to respond. They are able to stand side by side. There is a mutual give and take. We relinquish the need to be right. We eliminate the idea of ownership. There is mutuality and reciprocity in the relationship.

The notion of shared power with children is often a problem for parents. However, when children feel powerless, there are usually very negative consequences for both parents and children. While parents do need to operate from a position of authority, and are responsible for providing healthy structure and boundaries, they can, nonetheless, offer children age-appropriate areas of mutual power sharing.

7. Tenderness

Tenderness is demonstrated with physical affection. This is the kind of nonsexual physical touching we all need to thrive. There is nurturing touch that says, "I am here, you are not alone." "I offer my support." "Hello."

Tenderness is also expressed in words and attitude. It is so easy, after being with people for long periods of time, to let go of the little niceties we are so willing to offer to those we don't know as well. It is easy over time to take our partners, our parents, and even our friends for granted.

While the issue of safe sex is at the forefront of our thoughts today, the dynamics that create emotionally and spiritually safe sex also create physically safe sex. In other words, when you have an intimate adult-to-adult relationship built around spiritually and emotionally healthy guidelines, then physical sex becomes the culminating experience that binds two together.

8. Time

Relationships need time. When a group of 150 couples who lived together for over four years were asked how much time they spent with their partner each day, the answer was twenty-three minutes. Twenty-three minutes with the person each considered the most important to his or her life! People grow apart for many reasons, but for some it is as simple as getting caught up in other responsibilities and not taking time to "be" in a relationship. Valued relationships need time.

9. Long-Term Commitment

To have a healthy relationship we need to pay attention to the dynamics of it, and will make a commitment to working on our part. We trust that if there are problems in our relationship, the two of us will work them out. We trust that when there are problems, it does not mean the relationship is over.

When we have spent so much of our life in a survivorship mode, it is very easy for us to think of the "worst-case basis" when problems in our relationships arise. If the problem is with our partner, we may find ourselves automatically thinking of where we will go next, how we will support ourselves alone, and who else is or isn't "out there." We move into an all-or-nothing position, often beginning a defense against our incredible fear of rejection or abandonment. With our children, we may go into the "I'm a bad parent" orientation. While we may or may not physically abandon our children, we may not stay emotionally engaged. We forget we are their parent, and succumb to a helpless role, leaving the child to sort out situations for themselves. Healthy parenting also requires a commitment to stay involved.

Commitment does not mean you stay in a relationship irrespective of what may occur, though. At times, as people change, relationships are renegotiated. Commitments are reinforced or lessened, but when we make a commitment, we do what we can to make the relationship work, not allowing ourselves to be abused, nor allowing ourselves to give up our integrity in the process.

10. Forgiveness

There has to be room for forgiveness in any relationship. Forgiveness does not mean selling your heart and soul, or your integrity, to have peace. It means remembering and letting go. It is a cleansing of your pain and anger. It means maintaining your integrity while being able to let go.

"CHARTING" THE CHARACTERISTICS OF YOUR RELATIONSHIPS

Using these characteristics, the following are examples that may help you to reflect on how healthy you perceive yourself in specific relationships. Use the following form to "chart" your relationship characteristics. One means the least, and ten means the most.

Susan explored her relationship with her mother.

```
_____X_____    Respect
1   2   3   4   5   6   7   8   9   10
```

```
_____X_____    Honesty
1   2   3   4   5   6   7   8   9   10
```

```
                                               Realistic
_____X__       Expectations
1   2   3   4   5   6   7   8   9   10
```

```
_____X_____    Trust
1   2   3   4   5   6   7   8   9   10
```

```
_____X__    Autonomy
1   2   3   4   5   6   7   8   9   10


_____X__    Shared Power
1   2   3   4   5   6   7   8   9   10


_____X_____  Time
1   2   3   4   5   6   7   8   9   10

                                                 Long-Term
_____X__    Commitment
1   2   3   4   5   6   7   8   9   10


_____X__    Forgiveness
1   2   3   4   5   6   7   8   9   10
```

When Susan did this, she was actually surprised that all of her marks were in the high category. "I knew we had a healthy relationship, but it's not as close as this reflects." Remember, this reflects a healthy relationship, not necessarily closeness. Susan said, "Because of realistic expectations, I know what I can't get from my mother, and that's emotional openness on her part. She's very closed. Yet, I can enjoy her and I do appreciate her tenacity. I stay actively engaged in having a relationship with her."

The following example is Tom's reflection on how he sees himself to be relating with his oldest, his seventeen-year-old son.

```
___X_____    Respect
1   2   3   4   5   6   7   8   9   10


_____X_____    Honesty
1   2   3   4   5   6   7   8   9   10
```

			X							Realistic Expectations
1	2	3	4	5	6	7	8	9	10	

	X									Trust
1	2	3	4	5	6	7	8	9	10	

	X									Autonomy
1	2	3	4	5	6	7	8	9	10	

			X							Shared Power
1	2	3	4	5	6	7	8	9	10	

			X							Time
1	2	3	4	5	6	7	8	9	10	

						X				Long-Term Commitment
1	2	3	4	5	6	7	8	9	10	

			X							Forgiveness
1	2	3	4	5	6	7	8	9	10	

Clearly, this relationship is struggling. It takes a lot of self-honesty to benefit from this, but in doing so, Tom realized how angry he still was with his son for disappointing him by not actively pursuing a particular sport, football, and especially angry for his sensitivity and orientation to music. In doing this, Tom recognized the crux to establishing a better relationship with his son would be Tom's working on allowing autonomy and respecting his son for his uniqueness and individuality. He knew when he became more honest with himself, and then with his son about his own "image" of being an athlete, and took responsibility for some past pain in relationship to his childhood, he would be more forgiving and more willing to spend time to solidify a commitment he was only now beginning to acknowledge.

Helen chose to look at her relationship with her hairdresser, because Helen was not happy with how she was handling certain situations.

```
_____X__   Respect
1   2   3   4   5   6   7   8   9   10


_____X_____   Honesty
1   2   3   4   5   6   7   8   9   10

                                              Realistic
_____X_____   Expectations
1   2   3   4   5   6   7   8   9   10


_____N/A_____   Trust
1   2   3   4   5   6   7   8   9   10


_____X_____   Autonomy
1   2   3   4   5   6   7   8   9   10

_____X_____   Shared Power
1   2   3   4   5   6   7   8   9   10


_____N/A_____   Time
1   2   3   4   5   6   7   8   9   10

                                              Long-Term
_____X_____   Commitment
1   2   3   4   5   6   7   8   9   10
```

	N/A									Forgiveness
1	2	3	4	5	6	7	8	9	10	

In talking about her chart, Helen had no difficulty respecting her hairdresser. But when Helen was unhappy with the styling, she wouldn't tell the hairdresser, wanted the hairdresser to somehow just know, read her mind. Therefore, her realistic expectations were impaired. She was not owning her autonomy, taking her power and, as a result, she was not feeling a strong commitment.

Take time to explore your part of relationships in your life. At the back of this book, you will find a blank relationship chart you can copy.

Intimacy

In many of the families where we were raised, intimacies were often built upon lies and distortions. Usually family members do not have the skills for intimacy and even if they should, the nature of certain dysfunctions, such as addiction, interferes with such ability. As a result, people are very confused about the meaning of intimacy.

What does intimacy mean to you? How did you see it portrayed as a child? How is that still carried through in your behavior today?

— For John, as a child, intimacy was when his mother sobbed on his shoulder because his father had wrecked the car one more time.

— For Karen, intimacy was when her father came home six hours late, had missed her school event, but came into her room to tell her he loved her.

— Lou said intimacy was sex. It was only then that he remembers his mother wasn't crying and his father wasn't drinking.

— Vicky thought intimacy meant people being nice to each other. Being nice meant not arguing and not looking hostile.

— Jan said she thought intimacy was having a clean house.

— Bob said intimacy meant a loss of control.

— Bea said, "Intimacy means sharing with a friend or a partner.

How can you do that when you have shame? When you feel inadequate? You can't talk about yourself honestly. You can't show your feelings. You can't trust."

With perceptions as different as these, it is easy to see why people experience a struggle with intimacy. Bea's questions above are very significant. You will only be able to have the intimacy you so desire when you have addressed your primary issues first. You need to be able to separate your childhood fears from generalizing onto today's relationships. You need to have developed a sense of healthy boundaries. You need to come to like yourself and appreciate who you are. You need to be willing to take risks. You need to know what it is you feel, what it is you need, and to be able to communicate that. As you move forward in your recovery, your work will show itself in your relationships. All of the issues you have been working on contribute directly to a healthier way to be in a relationship.

As you commit to a relationship you are adding a room onto that home—will this be a continuation of the old beliefs, stories, secrecy? Or will your room have new furniture, fresh paint, with lots of windows and lighting?

We need to recognize that there are differences in who we were in our past and who we are today. Today you are a recovering person with many choices. You have the opportunity to develop clarity about what you value and like. You learn to identify your needs and feelings. You establish boundaries and set limits that create physical and psychological safety. You own the pain and shame of the past, and by putting it in its proper perspective, you don't project it onto others or maintain shields of armor, keeping people at a distance. You are developing the skills that will influence your choices of who you do and do not invite into your life, and skills that allow you much healthier ways of relating.

Intimacy is about being close. Intimacy is trusting another with who you are without the fear of rejection.

The different people we have relationships with are like characters in a play. Some will have minor roles and others, starring roles. Some will help to co-direct and co-produce our lives. They are all important to the overall play itself. We need to learn not to judge those who move in and out of the play, but to honor their appearance. Ultimately, we will look back on all of the people in our lives and realize we encountered them because they all had something to teach us.

7
Spirituality Is Something You Are

Forgiving, Loving, Finding Serenity

"Peace is not something you wish for. It is something you make, something you do, something you are, and something you give away."

—Mother Teresa

"Faith and control cannot peacefully co-exist."

—Claudia Black

When you set out on a new course in your life, the course of recovery, you are on a spiritual path; it is a path that leads to forgiving, accepting, loving, and finding serenity—within yourself and with others. This spiritual path promises to lead you from aloneness and emptiness to a sense of connection and meaning in your life.

On this new course, we are often involved in a process of spiritual growth before we recognize the spiritualness of it. Looking back, though, as we realized in the first chapter, the turning point came when we allowed ourselves to begin letting go of our fears and defenses to hear the truth:

There is another reality than the one I live. I want it.

This insight led us to learn more about the "other reality" and so learn more of the truth. The truth is that we are all human, both unique and ordinary, filled with dark and light. The truth is that all of our life experiences, whether admitted or denied, form the ground we stand on now. And the truth is that—in spite of our imperfections, our own and others' past errors, our past and present pain, and the roles we've adopted to survive—in spite of all this, we now know that we are truly free to choose how we live our own lives. Realizing this, the victim's passive plea, "Why me?" becomes a new, proactive question instead: "What can I do now?" This shift brings us to another turning point with another awareness:

I am responsible for the choices I make in my life.

When we accept our humanness and exercise our responsibility for making our own choices—for example, choosing what we do when we are angry, lonely, or sad—we are in a spiritual process. Our spirituality must be based on a vision that attends to our whole self and honors our whole experience, while at the same time, acknowledges that we are accountable in the present for our own feelings, beliefs, and behaviors.

In *The Spirituality of Imperfection,* Ernest Kurtz writes that we have suffered *zerrissenheit,* or "torn-to-pieces-hood." Spirituality, as he describes it, is the healing process of "making whole." "Spirituality helps us first to *see,* and then to *understand,* and eventually to *accept* the imperfection that lies at the core of our human *be*-ing."

Accepting our human limitations brings us inner peace. What a relief it is to put an end to the fight within ourselves! Also, as we find the permission to be the imperfect beings that we are, we become able to let others be who they are.

The experience of inner peace is foreign to those of us from shame-based families, because there was so little peace and harmony in our lives. We didn't have models that projected unconditional love, acceptance, or gratitude. As a result, we came to believe that if we were anything less than perfect, we were inferior, of little value. So we sought perfection, believing it was our only avenue to acceptance and love. We were so hurt by the absence of the nurturing we needed to thrive that we have spent a great portion of our lives trying to make that unconditional love happen in the present, hoping somehow to make up for the past. Paradoxically, when we are willing to believe that we cannot change the past, then we become willing to let go of our pain.

In earlier chapters, we compared a family to a house with many rooms. Our growing-up years were lived in our parents' room, which was connected to their parents' room, and their siblings' rooms, and so on. The present is the room where we have lived our adult lives. A mixture of experiences has taken place in all these rooms. Some experiences were good, some caused a lot of pain. We need to realize that all families are just as imperfect as all of us are as people. Those of us who don't understand or want to accept that truth must remain actively in denial. As Thomas Moore writes in *Care of the Soul,* "The sentimental image of family that we present publicly is a defense for the pain of proclaiming the family for what it is—a sometimes comforting, sometimes devastating house of life and memory."

To deny or disown any part of our experience leaves us dangerously incomplete and especially vulnerable to our shame. The lifeblood of shame is secrecy, fed by the dark fear of being found out. To grow toward wholeness in the context of our family home, we have to open all the doors and windows to let in air and light. Then, for us at last, healing will begin.

"You and I are children of mud, earthy and moist," Jane Smiley writes in *A Thousand Acres.* "We're not all fire and light—no matter how much we wish otherwise." Facing this truth, we reach another turning point:

It is in the acceptance of all that was and is that our spirits become whole.

Bill Moyers described acceptance as wholeness and health in an interview on his book, *Healing and the Mind:*

"Health is...a state of mind that recognizes the history of life, which includes moments of great delight and moments of deep sorrow. When we see all these parts of our being as connected, we come to terms with where we come from, who we are, and where we're going. Health is a whole."

In the process of becoming whole, we may say we "have spirituality." But spirituality, like recovery, isn't an event or a possession.

It's a way of living and being. Also, spirituality doesn't mean we never get hurt again, or that we are always smiling, always happy, never angry, and never scared. Spirituality in recovery does mean that when we are hurt or afraid, we can respond without making matters worse. Also, more and more as we change course and take steps on this spiritual road, we are able to enjoy the good feelings of being solidly balanced, open and unguarded, peaceful about the past, and generally positive about how we are living in the present.

SPIRITUALITY AND CONTROL

Spirituality must also be based on the acceptance of another awareness:

We are not "in control."

Sheldon Kopp says this another way: "No matter how well we may prepare, the moment belongs to God."

Accepting what we cannot control does not mean we give up all efforts to have order in our lives; we are not asked to thrive on chaos. We are asked only to give up the illusion that we can control what no one can. And, in accepting what we cannot control, we give up needlessly trying.

Because the whole notion of control is so clouded with anxiety and fear, let's try to clarify some issues: what we can and cannot control; our fears about losing control; and control versus surrender.

Learning What We Cannot Control

Some things are obviously out of our control—we can't make the sun come up or stop the rain. We can, however, build storm drains to channel the floods when the rain comes. But sometimes the waters rise too high, in spite of our best efforts, and houses are swept away. We are saddened by the loss, but we accept that we are not in control. We don't complicate our feelings with guilt or blame by thinking, "If only I had stopped the rain!"

In other aspects of our lives, control issues are easily confused. When we want something very much, we try very hard to get it or to make it happen. But, when we want something so much that we believe our lives depend on it, or our self-worth depends on it, then we believe we must make it happen. The belief "I must make it happen" implies that we *can* make it happen.

Control is very often confused in relationships. For instance, when someone believes, "I *must* have his or her love," it also seems logical to believe, "I must make him/her love me." Both beliefs are faulty—you will not die without the other's love, and you can't make a person love you any more than you can stop the rain. However, when caught up in the emotion of wanting something so much, it is understandable that people get confused.

Parents are probably second only to lovers when it comes to being confused about what they can control. "My child must be good..." "My child must study hard..." are beliefs that are followed by "... so I must make sure that happens." These outcomes can only be nurtured and encouraged, but not controlled.

What we can and cannot control is illustrated another way by Ernest Kurtz in *The Spirituality of Imperfection:*

We can control going to bed.	We cannot control sleeping.
We can control reading.	We cannot control understanding.
We can control executing a play.	We cannot control winning a game.
We can control knowledge.	We cannot control wisdom.

Learning to differentiate between what we can and cannot control is the first step to accepting our limitations. We are not God, we are not all-powerful—we are only humans and our power most definitely has limits.

Our Fears About Losing Control

As we consider giving up the idea of being in control, we are asking ourselves to have faith in something outside of our control. That, in and of itself, is a spiritual principle. Yet, being in control meant survival for so many of us. To manipulate people, places, and things brought order into our lives and offered the predictability we needed as children. When parents did not provide the structure that we needed, we attempted to provide it for ourselves. Being in control became a rigid form of protecting our Self.

Therefore, recognizing that we need to let go of control to truly experience spirituality is often what makes people stop in their tracks.

Whether we grew up in a chaotic or a rigid family environment, the world was a scary place, so for survival we learned ways of reacting to our experiences and to the people around us. We learned to shut down internally, to stop listening to our body, our physical sensations, and our emotions. These defenses blocked the natural tendency to be in tune with ourselves. We defended against our pain and shame externally with a variety of behaviors, ranging from compulsive busyness (work, hobbies, exercise) to social isolation, to the caretaking of others. Our responses to shame, ranging from control to perfectionism, from compulsive behaviors to chemical addiction—all are attempts to fill a spiritual void.

It is so important to have respect for doing what we needed to do to survive as children. Yet, today those old coping skills only get in our way. They create distance in our relationships. They interfere with enjoyment and fun.

Most importantly, control is a spiritual divider; it separates you from your spiritual self.

As we recognize life's open-endedness, we learn to be flexible and adaptable. In doing so, we are protected from the tendency to want to fix things, from our need to try to control the universe. This, in turn, offers us the opportunity to be at greater peace with the universe.

Control Versus Surrender

Spirituality is a surrendering process; surrendering the illusion that we must have all the answers, that we must be in charge so we can hide our shame. By becoming aware of the reality about what we are able to control, and by facing our old fears of being out of control, we become willing to surrender. We surrender to our inability to change the past and to our powerlessness to control the future. That leaves us with real life in the present. Living in the here and now is another fundamental spiritual concept.

Once again, the absence of being in total control does not mean we are asked to thrive on chaos, that we cannot try to have order in our lives, at least some order some of the time. We need to remember that our need to control usually comes from a basis of fear. It is often a response to shame, and operates from the motive that we need to try to control every aspect of our and everyone else's lives.

There is also the part of spirituality where we humbly ask a higher power for guidance. A higher power can be something outside of our self, or it can be our inner truth. Having faith, trusting in any person or concept outside of our own self when we were children, so focused on surviving, seemed like suicide.

People in recovery are survivors of pain, and many of them sense that if they surrender control to a higher power, they will lose themselves in the process. To them, surrender feels like becoming vulnerable to boundary violation again, and also vulnerable in the sense of losing protection against their pain.

Growing up in a troubled family has very often blocked our access to our spiritual self. Initially, our concept of a higher power, one whom we could supposedly trust, was learned from our interactions with our parents. Yet, these interactions most often taught us to not trust others, because even those closest to us could not be trusted. They made toxic decisions about the ways we were cared for, and did not have our best interests at heart. Those experiences generalized to a belief that if a higher power did exist, no trust was possible there, either.

In addition, when our sense of reality was continually invalidated, we learned not to trust the people who contradicted our internal messages. Even more devastating, we learned not to trust our own internal sensory experiences. Ultimately, we didn't even listen to the still, quiet voice from within.

When our earliest authorities, our parents, are incompetent, untrustworthy, or abusive, we learn not to respect or trust authority. For us, "authority" is feared. Authority, in our experience, uses power to control and/or punish. Obviously, we will resist the idea of surrendering to a higher power when it has a negative association with authority. To be open to believing in a higher power, we cannot conceive of the higher power as an authority that uses fear or control to influence.

SPIRITUALITY AND THE FEAR OF ABANDONMENT

Spirituality asks us to accept that there are many things we can't control. This acceptance includes surrendering our attachment to the outcome of those aspects of our lives we can't control. But what if everyone leaves us? Can we surrender our attachment to that outcome, which might mean the possibility of abandonment? To find the answer, we must deal with our own fear of abandonment.

Originally, our fear of abandonment was fear of death. As infants, if food, love, and nurture weren't provided, we would be crippled or die. However, as adults, since we can provide the necessities for ourselves, our fear of abandonment is, in reality, the fear of pain. "If I am abandoned emotionally, the pain will be so bad I'll go crazy," or "If no one loves me, I am worthless. Being worthless is so painful I may as well die."

When we have these fears, as everyone does from time to time, the important thing to remember is that, as part of our spiritual process, we are learning to accept ourselves. Through self-acceptance, we realize that our worth is not dependent on anyone else. This awareness brings us to another turning point:

I do not depend on others in order to accept myself.

This understanding is followed by another:

When people leave (abandon) me, it is not a judgment of my worth.

The truth is, any number of people may affirm us, but that will fall on deaf ears unless we accept and value ourselves.

We have come full circle. Our fear of abandonment can only be attended to and resolved by accepting ourselves. Conversely, if we don't accept ourselves and forgive our human limitations, we abandon ourselves.

SPIRITUALITY AND FORGIVENESS

Forgiving Ourselves

So far in this chapter, we have talked about accepting that which we can't control. However, accepting our imperfections sounds like a different matter. Imperfections mean that we don't always look as good as we want; we make mistakes that hurt others; we have secret fears that make us feel weak and secret desires that horrify us. How can we accept and forgive ourselves for these kinds of things?

To begin with, let's be clear that accountability and responsibility are not the same as forgiveness. We need to be accountable and responsible when we hurt others, and we need to make amends if possible. But then, we need to forgive ourselves for having made the mistake, for having blundered in our humanness again. While we may always regret what happened, we can still forgive ourselves. Forgiving means not hanging on to the shame, which is only more destructive in the end.

People have so much trouble forgiving themselves because they can't answer the question, "Why should I be forgiven?" To start with, we might ask ourselves, "Why shouldn't I?" Often, this reveals the belief that somehow we're supposed to punish ourselves because we're guilty. This idea usually comes from our religious or family background, something we've learned and internalized. We're not born with an internal judge of our badness. We deserve to go back to that more loving place in our earliest development, instead of hanging on to the hurt, judgment, and negativity around us.

When we can't seem to budge our resistance to forgiving ourselves, another question to ask is, "What do I get out of maintaining the belief that I'm not okay, or that I'm bad?" Also, it is humbling to forgive ourselves—maybe we don't feel okay being humble because humility is confused with being weak.

The opposite of "to forgive" is "to condemn." Whatever we condemn, we don't accept. In our acceptance and forgiveness, we learn to say, again and again:

I forgive myself for what I did to survive.

I forgive myself for continuing to make mistakes.

Forgiving Others

In accepting our own limitations we also learn to accept the imperfections of others. Forgiveness of others is a powerful manifestation of a spiritual connection. Many people on their course to family healing are able to understand why certain things occurred in the past, and in their recovery process, they are able to come to a place of forgiveness in their heart. But others struggle much more with forgiveness—often those who experienced greater shame and pain at the hands of abusers.

People healing from family wounds become very confused about forgiveness, feeling there is a strong "should" attached to it, believing they "should" be able to forgive. This belief carries a message of good or bad and right or wrong. You are good if you forgive, bad if you do not. You are right if you forgive; you are wrong if you do not.

Other messages are implied when you believe you should forgive, but don't feel ready to do so. One implication is that you are angry, and as such, you are bad and wrong. Another implication is that you are putting your priorities over others and that too is bad and wrong. We need to let go of our "should's." Forgiveness is not about being good or bad, right or wrong. This is about being true to yourself.

Whether or not you are able to forgive others should not be the focus of treatment or recovery. Forgiveness is something you may ask for yourself; it is something you may pray to be able to give others. However, you may still be angry and hurt, and not ready to truly forgive. While it is not a goal of recovery, for many forgiveness is a gift that may come.

Only in knowing what forgiveness means to you can you put it into a healing perspective. The following are thoughts that I believe may be helpful to you as you sort through your feelings and come to terms with the role forgiveness has in your healing. By recognizing what forgiveness is *not*, it is more possible to see what forgiveness *is*.

What Forgiveness Is Not

...Forgiveness is not forgetting.

We cannot forget what has happened, nor should we. Past experiences, and even the pain, have a great deal to teach us about not being victimized again and about not victimizing others.

...Forgiveness is not condoning.

By forgiving the people who hurt us, we are not saying that what was done to us was acceptable, or unimportant, or "not so bad." It was important. It hurt, and it has made a difference in our lives.

...Forgiveness is not absolution.

Forgiving others does not absolve them; it doesn't "erase" what they have done. They are still responsible for the harm they caused.

...Forgiveness is not a form of self-sacrifice.

In forgiving, we are not swallowing our true feelings; forgiving does not mean playing martyr. There is a real difference between repressing a feeling and releasing a feeling.

...Forgiveness doesn't mean we are never angry again about what occurred.

What happened to us was hurtful. It was not right; it was not fair. For that we may always feel anger. We have every reason and right to be angry. But we want to get to a point that our anger no longer interferes with how we care about ourselves or how we live our lives.

...Forgiveness doesn't happen by making a one-time decision.

No matter how sincerely we want to let go of the past and move on with our life, we cannot just wave a magic wand and, in one moment, blithely make the past disappear. There is a process of grief work which we must walk through that allows forgiveness to occur.

What Forgiveness Is

...Forgiveness is recognizing we no longer need our grudges and resentments, our hatred, and self-pity.

We do not need these negative emotions as excuses for getting less out of life than we want or deserve. We do not need them as a weapon to hurt those who hurt us or to keep other people from getting close enough to hurt us again.

...Forgiveness is no longer wanting to punish the people who hurt us.

Realizing that we can never truly "even the score," forgiveness is the inner peace we feel when we stop trying to.

...Forgiveness is no longer building an identity around something that happened to us in the past.

We realize that there is more to us than our past. The past is put into its proper perspective as one part of who we are in the present.

...Forgiveness is what happens naturally as a result of con-

fronting past painful experiences and healing old wounds.

...Forgiveness is an internal process. It happens within.

...Forgiveness is a moral right, not a moral obligation.

...Forgiveness is remembering and letting go.

For most people, forgiveness is something that occurs gradually, over time. As the work of recovery and healing takes place, anger and hurt are often replaced by forgiveness and deeply felt spiritual acceptance. With every tear that is shed and every cry of rage that is released, more room is opened for forgiveness to enter the heart.

As you do the work of healing, forgiveness will naturally begin to manifest itself in your life by degrees. What is necessary for healing is a commitment to healing; forgiveness will then take care of itself.

For those of you who have been abused, the only forgiveness you need for yourself is the forgiveness from yourself. You were a child. You did not have the power to respond any differently than you did. You were not bad or evil. You were not then and you are not today. Your body may have been violated; your emotions may have been repressed and turned inward; your view of yourself may be filled with fear, shame, grief, and rage. Still, your spirit remains unspoiled and whole. No matter what your experience has been, your spirit remains beautifully free of it all.

Ultimately, it is your own powerful spirit that will heal you. Though we speak of body, mind, and emotions as distinct entities, they are inseparable; what effects one, affects the others. The spirit, however, stands free and possesses a powerful force for healing.

SPIRITUALITY AND OUR RELIGIOUS UPBRINGING

Unfortunately, our experiences with religion have very likely created conflict within us that interferes with our openness to a spiritual path. All too often, we feel very alone and confused, seemingly betrayed by the only higher power we have ever known.

For most of us, that higher power was steeped in the definitions of a particular religion. Based on that religion, we were taught the Golden Rule to "Do unto others as you would have them do unto you." Be loving. Respect your parents. Be honest. Do not lie.

In many troubled families, however, children often found a contradiction between the religious teachings they were taught and what happened in their daily lives. Instead of respect, they heard verbal abuse. Instead of loving behavior, they saw one parent cause another intense anger or sadness. Instead of honesty, they witnessed their parents lie, or they were even asked or told to lie for a family member under the guise of "protection." How many times did you and all the others in the family keep going to church, getting all dressed up, putting on your smiles, lying about why Mom or Dad wasn't there, saying they were sick, when Dad was too hung over to get out of bed, or Mom didn't come home, or Mom was still bruised from Dad? How many times did you go home from church to neglect, abuse, addiction kept hidden from the world?

Most children of troubled families truly believed in the higher power, as it was portrayed in their house of worship, but the contradiction of the religious messages with their family lives was too great for their continued commitment.

When you were growing up, how many times did you pray asking...

...for Dad to come home, but he didn't.

...for Mom to be on time, but she was always late.

...for Dad to stop hitting Mom, but he wouldn't.

...for Dad to leave and never come back, but he stayed.

...for Mom to protect you, but she didn't.

...for Mom and Dad to be happy, but they never were.

...to take away the abuse, the neglect, the illnesses, the hurts, disappointments, but they continued.

After feeling abandoned by our parents, feeling that God had not answered our prayers was, for many of us, the ultimate abandonment experience.

Spiritual Abuse

Spiritual pessimism and, in fact, even spiritual abuse were often created by religions that try to control us by generating fear that we are evil or bad, and that we may lose our souls. Great numbers of unsuspecting, trusting people have experienced spiritual abuse caused by harmful beliefs that were couched in a religious framework. These were beliefs that fueled fear, unworthiness, guilt, and shame. For people with such experiences, it will be necessary to review their religious beliefs to determine whether these have been spiritually nourishing or spiritually abusive.

Even more extreme are situations where parents use their religious beliefs or practices as a way to directly, or indirectly, control their children. Phyllis ultimately had to deal with the pain associated with her father always being away from home, attending to his "flock," while she and five other children were left home alone with a raging alcoholic mother. When Phyllis was angry, periodically, and yelled at her father to bring his attention to the pain going on at home and the fact that he was needed at home by his children, she was told to pray for forgiveness to the Almighty. To be angry was perceived as a sin. All painful feelings, particularly anger, were seen as being separate from God. To express that anger at an authority was a greater sin. To put your needs ahead of others (Dad's parishioners) was a higher sin.

In Phyllis's case, religious beliefs were used to induce guilt and shame, and in so doing, indirectly controlled her life. In John's experience, the issue of control was very direct. John was forced to read the Old Testament repeatedly, and then was quizzed by either his mother or father before being able to spend time with friends. John was told it was the Bible that would dispense rewards. As a consequence, it was the Bible that was to become his punishing stick.

These cases of abuse associated with religion were not really religious practices advocated by a church's doctrine. These were abuses by very hurtful, frightened, shameful, controlling adults who used aspects of their religion to control and manipulate young children. Yet, when these same children become adults, it is often the religious doctrine they are angry with, not the people who framed it to suit their purpose.

Without addressing their spiritual abuses in the past, these people will continue to struggle with contradictory experiences. It will be important for them to sort out "the messenger from the message." It will be important to develop a relationship with a doctrine whose beliefs don't foster punishment and shame. We do not deserve to live in fear of a wrathful and punishing God, but to believe in the good of all, and that includes ourselves.

Believing that our prayers were not heard, or even worse, believing that our prayerful pleas for help were ignored, created spiritual conflict within us. Having our parents use religious beliefs or practices to punish, humiliate, or control us, and/or having experienced direct harm by those "of the church" in their attempts to control or humiliate us into obedience, also leads to spiritual conflict. We feel abandoned by our parents, possibly by our church, and as we said earlier, ultimately abandoned by God. In addition to feeling abandoned and hurt, we may be angry with our parents, the church, and also with God. Just owning the possibility that you are angry with God may be very frightening for you.

If you are angry, you need to acknowledge it and externalize it. This is often the first step in clearing the way to a spiritual path that will help you to come to peace with your past. A helpful technique for expressing your anger and rage is to write a letter to God. In your letter, tell God why you are angry. People sometimes feel uncomfortable doing this, but remember that when you release pent-up anger and rage, relief and reconciliation will follow.

Making An Inventory Of Religion And Spirituality In Your Past

While religion and spirituality are not necessarily one and the same, it may be helpful to explore your childhood history, to help understand how your experiences with religion may be impacting your concept of spirituality. Here are some questions to give thought to, to write, or talk to someone about:

1. Were you forced to attend church (synagogue) as a child, or otherwise participate in religious practices? If your involvement in your church or synagogue ended, what made you stop? If you didn't attend any type of church, how was that decision made?

2. If you were involved in a church, or a religious group, describe your experience. Fun? Scary? Boring? Hopeful? Meaningful?

3. What was your concept of a Higher Power (God)? Loving? Punishing? Indifferent? Other_____?

4. Were there any particular rituals or ceremonies that were of special value or significance for you? What were they? How were they special?

5. Looking back at your early religious influence, what aspects were positive that are still with you today? Are there any negative influences that are still with you?

It is not uncommon for people to return (or if they didn't leave it, they engage more positively) to the faith and church of their youth, while many others choose a different faith or church. Some decide to follow a guru. Others decide to follow the Earth religions. Many people practice Twelve Step concepts. It has been reported that the Twelve Step programs, beginning with Alcoholics Anonymous in 1935, are the largest spiritual (not religious) movement in the United States. In recovery, every spiritual door is open.

Again, for the sake of clarity, spirituality is not a religion. Spirituality is not a framework for a set of beliefs. Religion is a set of beliefs that follows from a central belief in God or a Higher Power, and a set of practices which arises out of those beliefs. Religion can be a bridge to the spiritual. Spirituality may be an integral part of a religion. However, organized religion does not necessarily include spirituality.

SPIRITUALITY AND THE SPIRIT OF OUR INNER CHILD

Until we were told what we should and shouldn't feel, or given ways to redefine our experiences, our earliest spiritual experiences were all natural. Children are authentic, and spirituality is about being authentic in the way we exist. Children are naturally present in the moment. They are in tune with and entranced by the mysterious life that they embody. Children have a natural affinity for the earth, seen by their sitting on the ground, rolling down hills, etc. They feel a connectedness to the elements—the wind, the sky, animals, the trees. Until taught otherwise, children believe the world is their friend. They are curious and receptive to its ever-changing flow of events.

The authentic, uncensored, connected child is the Natural Child, the child who still lives within each of us. It is the spirit of our Inner Child.

Our Inner Child consists of our intuitiveness, spontaneity, our vitality. It is the part of us that is naturally open and trusting, until it learns to shut down for self-protection. It is emotionally expressive, until it is criticized. It is playful, until its spirit is crushed for being exuberant. It is creative, until ridiculed. We often bury our Inner Child, ignore it, distort it, or medicate it, but our Inner Child is our spirit that remains with us. When we become disconnected from our Inner Child, we lose much of the mystery and magic of life. We lose the delight of intimacy; we lose our spiritual self.

Another way to describe our Inner Child is to recognize it as the cognitive framework for our vulnerable self. Also, it is that part of our self that knows what we feel and what we need. Referring to our vulnerable self as our Inner Child is a way to access or get in touch with this knowing.

Sometimes, in order to get in touch with our Inner Child, we have to go back and undo messages that our rational self has learned that now obscure our tenderest feelings deep inside. We have to get in touch with those feelings, though, in order to open up to our spirit within. Just as a dark, secret room in our family house is a metaphor for a shameful secret, so is our Inner Child a metaphor for the softest, most natural feelings we hold inside. For the life-breath of spirituality to move throughout our lives, we must open all the avenues to all the protected and vulnerable places within us; we must open up and connect with our Inner Child.

When you have a hard time accessing your Inner Child, think about something or someone for whom you have unconditional love; your child (especially as a baby) or your pet, your cat or dog. Using your dog as an example, when he is playful, do you think of calling him foolish? When he barks in fear, do you believe he is stupid or cowardly for being afraid? Can you tap into the sense that for your pet, there are no "should"s or "shouldn't"s for its feelings and behaviors. Therefore, your pet lives free of judgment or shame. Now, are you willing to offer yourself that same freedom?

In doing Inner Child work, you will come to identify several different aspects of your Inner Child. Often there is the Victim Child, who says, "I am helpless! I need someone else to do it for me." Or the Frightened Child, who says, "Go away! I don't need you!" Or the Angry Child, who says, "Where have you been? You left me all alone! I don't want you now!" It can be helpful to attach different names to the different experiences of our vulnerable self. In doing so, it gives us a framework to get in touch with how vulnerable we have been and often still are.

As you come to know different aspects of your Inner Child, try to recognize that these different aspects are protectors of the Innocent, Natural Child. When your Natural Child was not being nurtured, heard, and supported, you created other aspects of your Inner Child that offered a form of protection to your true self. Therefore, as you are doing your healing work, it is only natural that you will uncover the pain of the Wounded Child. Much of what you hear from your inner self is the voice of the Wounded, Abandoned Child—its fear, anger, grief and pain. You may have to spend months being present for your Wounded Child in a loving way before some of the inner pain begins to heal. As that pain begins to melt away, your protector selves will begin to relax, which in turn will clear the way for the Natural Child to emerge.

Songwriter and singer, Lynn Bosworth, reflects the spirit of the child in the song, "A Child Knows."

A child knows, a child knows....
A child knows, a child knows.
A child hears the wind sing;
A child knows the earth's a living thing.

A child sees the leaves dance;
A child knows, there is no second chance.
Live right now, live right now.
Dance right now, sing right now.
Raise your hands and your voice to the wonder of it all.

Healing is about learning to connect with and to love our natural self. Rejecting the child within us is another way to reject our selves and to abandon the care of our inner spirit.

PRACTICING SPIRITUALITY

Spirituality acknowledges and does homage to the spark of divinity within each of us; it is an approach to life, an attitude. As we grow spiritually, we learn to trust that life will continue to unfold as it must, but we will remain spiritually whole, grounded in our authenticity, and centered in our openness to learning. To grow spiritually we must "walk the talk." Practicing spirituality means that we:
- do the footwork;
- be present, be in the here and now;
- stay attuned to our inner guidance;
- be authentic;
- put forth the effort;
- let go of the attachment to the results; and,
- believe in the divine guidance and choice it offers.

Spirituality must be lived, practiced consistently, and acted on consciously. The spiritual path is a commitment to personal transformation, to service, and to not harming others. This commitment shows itself most clearly in a person's attitude toward life. Our personal spirituality is a blend of our intent to be authentic and our openness to our intuition. From this foundation follows a willingness to trust, to be tolerant and gentle, and a willingness to continue learning from life.

The practice of spirituality embraces gratitude as an attitude that is both a measure of our happiness and a reminder to find our happiness. It is being grateful for what we do have, instead of regretting what we do not have. We learn tolerance and acceptance of both likenesses and differences. It recognizes and understands that we all struggle with the same fears and sorrows, and we all do the best we can with what we have.

Practicing spirituality in our lives finds us taking time daily to honor our humanness, to appreciate the universe, and to give and share with others. Selfless service is a spiritual practice, but must be distinguished from the guilty need to rescue. Selfless service, or service from the self, comes not from need, but from compassion. In spiritual practice, what we offer to others is freely and spontaneously given. It comes from our heart, without expectation of return. In service, we feel the truth that "to give is to receive." Spirituality is an ability to accept love, as well as the capacity to give love. It is an instinctive empathy, an act of kindness, generosity, intuitive thoughtfulness.

Recovery changes the course of our search for serenity from the outer world to the inner one. Our true self cannot be discovered from the outside. Our beingness can only be discovered in the silence of our inner life. We access our real identity when our mind becomes quiet and we are fully conscious and present in the moment.

A common symptom of modern life is that there is no time for thought, or even for letting the impressions of a day sink in. Yet even the simplest act of pausing offers a period of non-doing that is essential nourishment of the spirit. Washing dishes is no less an invitation to a holy moment than is a sunset. Listening to friends, playing with children, stroking our pets, sharing from the heart; these are ways that we naturally center. Similar to pausing, and just as important in the care of the spirit, is the practice of taking "time out." The spirit basks in the extended sense of time. Setting aside time is the spiritual practice that supports all other spiritual works.

The world is filled with noise and distractions, from television to social chatter to unbidden thoughts. It is important to develop a process of turning off the external noise and tuning in the internal voice, the still quiet voice within. Warren E. Oates described this as "nurturing silence in a noisy heart."

There is no one right way to practice this. You might find that setting aside time at sunset to watch the changing colors, to feel the changing atmosphere, to hear the sounds at dusk, and breathe in tune with the experience, will take you right into that quiet place inside where you commune with that which is holy.

Spiritual development requires spiritual practice, just as the person who wants to be physically fit must exercise. Without the workouts—nothing happens. If you set your course toward inner calm and peace of mind, daily spiritual practice is necessary.

Spirituality is a process of going inward to the part of yourself that is connected to the larger context. Some of the spiritual practices to connect with your inner life are:

• prayer
• meditation
• practice of silence/quietness
• guided imagery
• living a "thought"-full life

As you engage in spiritual practice, the location, the sounds, the time, the use of materials—books, for example—often become significant, meaningful parts of your ritual. Many people include rituals involving deep breathing and relaxation. By definition, spirituality is derived from the Latin word *spiritus,* which means "the act of breathing." Breathing allows you to be open within your own body, to go "inside." Once your physical body is relaxed, it is necessary to relax your mind and let go of thoughts and worries.

Prayer is common in religious services in the church, the ashram, or the temple, it is also an important part of spiritual practice throughout the day. Some people have a favorite meditation book, and include reading from it during times of prayer. Some people get on their knees; others have a sitting area where they are surrounded by favorite objects, photographs, and plants. Prayer and/or meditation is something you can do while sitting in your living room, lying in your bed, walking along the beach, or jogging in the park. Both prayer and meditation are practices that nurture and develop our connection to self and spirit. Prayer is an act that puts us in touch with the power greater than all else.

For many people, particularly those who have used keeping busy as a form of self-protection, the idea of meditation is particularly frightening. The idea of doing what appears to be "nothing" or "just being" is difficult to comprehend. Yet, it is meditation that allows you to completely stop, to let go of thoughts about the immediate past or future, and simply focus on being in the here and now.

SPIRITUALITY, THE TURNING POINT TO A NEW COURSE

For so many of us, our entire lives have been about reacting, surviving, and being vigilant to the outside forces. We deserve the "other reality" we want. Many of us are used to being in control, and want recovery now, so we try to skip over the emotional work and go directly to the promised spiritual realm. Others of us attempt to find inner peace and harmony from an intellectual understanding, or do volunteer work to demonstrate our spiritual intent. While any sincere effort can be extremely valuable, we cannot singularly "will" ourselves to a higher plane. We cannot skip the steps. We cannot be spiritual people unless we do the necessary work. Part of the work on ourselves is to understand our past and present relationship with a higher power. We can do that only when we take time out to listen to our own internal processes. When we can hear our heart and soul, we experience our spiritual truth.

Becoming whole requires a journey into and through the darkness of the wounds of childhood and healing our child within. When we begin to experience the world as less frightening, we know we can take care of ourselves; we know we have the inner resources to make it; we do not have to live in hypervigilance any longer. We can say "no" to our shame. Doing these things, we move beyond the confines of the past on to a course of spirituality in the present.

We deserve the journey inward. In *Dialogue with Hasidic Tales,* Maurice Friedman relates the Hasidic belief that if we want to change from one reality to another, we must go through a "between-stage" in which we must first change into a blank slate. In this stage we experience a "holy despair," when we know that no other help can come except that which comes from God. When we accept that we cannot be God ourselves, that is the turning point of our recovery. When we come to believe that God, the Higher Power, is all around us and also within us, that is the turning point of our spirituality.

Some of us have experienced these turning points through our houses of worship. Others of us find it in nature, in song, or the power of a group.

But God is always present in the heart.
Look within.

Turning Points

1. There is another reality than the one I live. I want it.

2. I am willing to take some risks to have it.

3. If you have pain, you deserve to heal.

4. If you have anger or guilt from the past, you deserve to heal.

5. If you are protecting yourself from past pain in ways that are causing you even more pain in the present, you deserve to heal.

6. The pain we feel is not only from the past, but also from the past-driven present.

7. We were powerless in the past, but we are not powerless in the present.

8. We are not our pain.

9. Our pain is our responsibility.

10. What we do about our pain is a choice we make.

11. Recovery isn't changing who you are. It is letting go of who you are not.

12. To say, "I did not learn this very basic skill and I need to know how" is a turning point.

13. You have the opportunity to turn now.

14. You deserve to begin rebuilding your life in a new direction.

15. Recovery is learning the numbers two through nine.

16. By recognizing that you are in the process of recovery, you are beginning to shine your own light.

17. Learning to love yourself does not mean you love others less. Instead, it frees you to love them more.

18. A turning point will come when you can identify a safe way to share the secret.

19. The awareness that now you can choose to be free from the secret is a turning point.

20. The awareness that we have adopted a protective role is a turning point.

21. The awareness that we no longer need that role to survive is a turning point.

22. The turning point in your relationship is the awareness that your growth is not about getting other people to change.

23. Confrontation offers the opportunity for closure. You have choices. You are not a coward if you choose not to confront face-to-face.

24. Intimacy is about being close. Intimacy is trusting another with who you are without the fear of rejection.

25. I am responsible for the choices I make in my life.

26. It is in the acceptance of all that was and is that our spirits become whole.

27. We are not "in control."

28. I do not depend on others in order to accept myself.

29. When people leave (abandon) me, it is not a judgment of my worth.

30. God is always present in the heart. Look within.

Appendices

A. Loss Graph For Early Years

B. Loss Graph For Adult Years

C. "Charting" Your Relationships

Loss Graph For Early Years

Loss Events: _____

Age:

Unattended
Feelings:

Loss Conditions	Abandonment
in Family: _____	Experiences/Feelings: _____
_____	_____
_____	_____

Loss Graph For Adult Years

Loss Events: _____

Age:

Unattended
Feelings:

Loss Conditions   Abandonment
in Family: _____   Experiences/Feelings: _____

_____   _____

_____   _____

"Charting" Your Relationships

————————————————————————— Respect
1   2   3   4   5   6   7   8   9   10

————————————————————————— Honesty
1   2   3   4   5   6   7   8   9   10

————————————————————————— Realistic Expectations
1   2   3   4   5   6   7   8   9   10

————————————————————————— Trust
1   2   3   4   5   6   7   8   9   10

————————————————————————— Autonomy
1   2   3   4   5   6   7   8   9   10

————————————————————————— Shared   Power
1   2   3   4   5   6   7   8   9   10

————————————————————————— Time
1   2   3   4   5   6   7   8   9   10

————————————————————————— Long-Term Commitment
1   2   3   4   5   6   7   8   9   10

————————————————————————— Forgiveness
1   2   3   4   5   6   7   8   9   10

Also by Claudia Black, Ph.D.

My Dad Loves Me, My Dad Has A Disease
It Will Never Happen To Me
Repeat After Me
It's Never Too Late To Have A Happy Childhood
(Ballantine Random House)
Double Duty (Ballantine Random House)

Books, Videos, Audiocassettes
by
Claudia Black
available through

MAC Publishing
5005 E. 39th Avenue
Denver, Colorado 80207
Phone: (303) 331-0148
Fax: (303) 331-0212

To arrange a speaking engagement by Dr. Black,
please contact the address below:

Claudja, Inc.
321 High School Road, #346
Bainbridge Island, WA 98110
Phone: (206) 842-6303
Fax: (206) 842-6235